Another Can of Worms

by Debbie Caffrey

Published by
Debbie's Creative Moments, Inc.
PO Box 29418
Santa Fe, NM 87592-9418

www.debbiescreativemoments.com

Credits

Written and Illustrated by

Debbie Caffrey
Santa Fe, New Mexico

Quilts Photographed by

Dan Caffrey
President of Everything
Debbie Doesn't Want to Do
Santa Fe, New Mexico

Detail Images Photographed by

Debbie Caffrey
Santa Fe, New Mexico

Proofread by

Erin Caffrey
Nashville, Tennessee

Printed by

Palmer Printing
St. Cloud, Minnesota

Quilts Designed and Pieced by

Debbie Caffrey
Santa Fe, New Mexico

All Quilts Machine Quilted by

Phyllis Kent
Los Lunas, New Mexico

Published by

Debbie's Creative Moments, Inc.
P. O. Box 29418
Santa Fe, NM 87592-9418
USA
www.debbiescreativemoments.com

ISBN: 0-9645777-9-8

First Printing, 2006

Another Can of Worms

©2006 by Debbie Caffrey

Other Books by Debbie Caffrey

Power Cutting, Too

Power Cutting

~~*Shape Up Your Fat Quarters*~~
Sorry, this one is out of print.

Noodle Soup

Open a Can of Worms

Quilting Season

Scraps to You, Too

~~*Blocks & Quilts Everywhere!*~~
Sorry, this one is out of print.

An Alaskan Sampler

Patterns by Debbie Caffrey

Debbie publishes a growing line of *Classy Patterns*. These quilt patterns are full color updated patterns inspired by classic designs, and constructed with modern, efficient techniques. Many include photographs similar to those you find in this book. All are written with the professional, detailed instructions that you find in all of her books.

Table of Contents

What is a Worm?

And, what does it have to do with quilting?

A *worm* **is a strip of fabric that is cut 2½″ wide, selvage to selvage, making it approximately 42″ long with selvages on each of the short ends.**

Sometime in the mid-1990's I began to cut my short pieces of fabric leftovers into strips of various widths. I realized that I could locate my small pieces if they were organized by size rather than only by color. Another realization was that not only could I find the small pieces of fabrics, but because they were already cut into pieces of uniform sizes, I could stack them and cut scrap quilts in record time.

Then, I found the tools on the notions wall at the quilt shop! Most of their cutting techniques begin with a strip. The tools are used to cut pieces from the strip – pieces like half-square triangles, quarter-square triangles, trapezoids, equilateral triangles, almost any shape you can use in your quilt. The discovery of the abundance of tools created many options beyond basic strip-pieced quilts.

Well, once I began to slice and dice the strips, the quilts just would not stop coming. I thought that I could make quilts from strips forever and not run out of ideas. I had truly *opened a can of worms*. In 2000 I stopped making quilts from my worms long enough to write the first book of patterns and techniques using 2½″ wide strips, *Open a Can of Worms*. It is in its fifth printing at the time I am writing this book and continues to be my best selling book even now. The time has come to reveal more quilts made from worms, so here is a sequel to *Open a Can of Worms*.

About This Book

This book contains four more quilts and five more patterns than the first book.

One big change for this book is that the quilts were designed in pairs. I continue to teach "worms" across the country, and I hear comments from quilters who love the patterns, but they do not necessarily want to make all of them scrappy quilts. So, in this book you will find eight pairs of quilts. The fabric requirement for the second variation, which immediately follows the first, has been simplified. Also, the setting for the second quilt of each pair is usually very different from the setting of the first. *Open a Can of Worms* provides you with a good number of border options. Consider mixing and matching parts of quilts from both books, e.g., the setting for a quilt in this book with the border of a quilt in *Open a Can of Worms*, to make even more quilts.

Another change in this book is that the cutting information is not in a section all by itself. Cutting techniques are described within the pattern where they are first used. I struggled with the decision because I want to teach you how to quilt, not provide recipes to make quilts. Realize that these techniques are skills you can use to make an endless number of quilts and not specific to the one pattern where they are detailed. It is a good idea to read through all of the patterns to familiarize yourself with all of the cutting techniques.

Those of you familiar with *Open a Can of Worms* know that there is a section at the end of each pattern entitled "Options to Consider". The section contains brief information about enlarging the quilt to a queen size and suggests other uses for the pattern. The format in this book is slightly different. The first pattern of each pair is followed by a section which contains information about enlarging the quilt to a queen size. The second pattern of each pair does not have multiple sizes. Omitting the multiple sizes for all quilts allowed me to include more patterns for you. Remember, I want you to learn to quilt not just follow recipes. With that in mind, consider the *Autumn Evening* quilt on page 16. It is a small quilt made with eight blocks set on point. Now, look at *Happy Talk* on page 47. It is a quilt made with thirty-two blocks set on point. One way to enlarge *Autumn Evening* is to make four times as many blocks and set the blocks as shown in *Happy Talk*. Changing the size of a quilt can be just that easy! Even when you use a recipe from a cookbook you must adjust the measurements to make the number of portions you need. All of you are familiar with doubling ingredients to make twice as much when you cook. Quilting works the same way. You just use different ingredients.

I will not spend time in this book duplicating details about fabric selection, preparing fabrics, cutting strips, quilting, binding, or other basic skills. These basic skills have entire books dedicated solely to them. They are a part of every quilt. Learn to do them well. My books *Power Cutting* and *Power Cutting Too* are great resources for learning efficient and precise rotary cutting techniques.

Just a Few Last Details

Most of the fabric requirements list "worms" as an item. Remember, a worm is a strip of fabric 2½″ x approximately 42″. So, if a pattern requires eighteen worms, you need a total of eighteen strips. I used one strip each of eighteen different fabrics in such a project. You may choose to use two strips each of nine fabrics or three strips each of six fabrics, and so on.

A half-strip, a piece that is 2½″ x approximately 21″ and usually cut from fat quarter leftovers, is suitable for many of the quilts. You need thirty-six half-strips for a quilt that requires eighteen worms.

You will see small arrows in most of the pattern illustrations. These arrows indicate the directions for pressing the seam allowances.

Finally, I would like to share two important attributes of accurate piecing. The first is sewing precision. The success of your quilt depends upon accurate ¼″ seam allowances throughout. At the right end of each strip-pieced panel you will find a measurement. That measurement is what your panel should measure after it has been stitched and pressed. If yours are not accurate, adjust your seam allowance and restitch.

Secondly, I do not square up! I cut accurately, sew accurately, and move on to the next quilt.

Now, let's slice some worms!

Sand and Sea
61″ x 78½″

Sand and Sea

Sand and Sea and *Sweet Sixteen* are two quilts based on a traditional Sixteen Patch block.

Finished Size of Quilt – 61″ x 78½″
Finished Size of Block – 8″

Fabric Requirements

35 Tan Worms

35 Dark Worms (greens and blues)

Sashing	1⅞ yards
Binding	¾ yard
Backing	4¾ yards

Cutting

All seventy of the worms are cut exactly the same way. Cut carefully. There is little excess fabric.

Cut the following from **each** strip:
two 2½″ x 8½″ rectangles for the border blocks, and
reserve the remainder of the strip for strip-piecing the Sixteen Patch blocks.

Piecing the Blocks

Sixteen Patch Blocks

Select the remainder of one tan and one dark strip to make one Sixteen Patch block. Sew the strips together along one long edge. Press the seam allowances toward the dark strip. Cut the strip-pieced section in half. See figure 1.

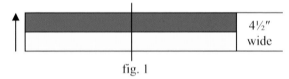

4½″ wide

fig. 1

Sew the two halves together to make a panel (figure 2). Press the seam allowances toward the dark. This panel should measure 8½″. If it does not, adjust your seam allowance and restitch. Crosscut the panel into four sections that are 2½″ wide.

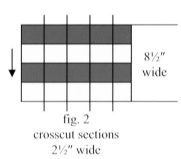

8½″ wide

fig. 2
crosscut sections
2½″ wide

Rotate the second and fourth sections 180°. Sew the sections together to complete a Sixteen Patch block (figure 3). Press the seam allowances to one side.

Repeat with the remaining fabrics to make a total of thirty-five blocks.

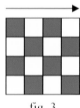

fig. 3
make 35 blocks

Border Blocks

Use four light 2½″ x 8½″ rectangles to piece a block like the one shown on the left in figure 4. Press the seam allowances to one side. Repeat to make sixteen light border blocks. Use the dark rectangles to piece sixteen dark border blocks. Press the seam allowances to one side.

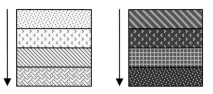

fig. 4
make 16 of each block

Corner Blocks

Make the corner blocks using a sew & flip method. Place two light border blocks on top of each other, right sides together. The seam lines should be on top of one another and the seam allowances should nest together. If the seam allowances of both blocks are going the same way, fix it in one of these two ways: press the seam allowances of the top block in the opposite direction or rotate the top block 180°. Stitch the pair of blocks along one diagonal as shown by the dashed line in figure 5. Check your work. If it looks like the completed block on the right in figure 5, trim the excess, as shown by the solid line, leaving ¼″ for seam allowances.

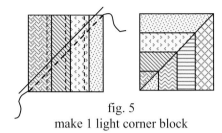

fig. 5
make 1 light corner block

Repeat the instructions directly above using two dark border blocks to make a block like the one shown in figure 6.

Use one light and one dark border block and the sew & flip technique to piece a corner block like the one shown on the left in figure 7. Use one light and one dark border block to piece a corner block like the one shown on the right in figure 7. ***NOTE: The two blocks in figure 7 are the reverse of each other. Check your work before trimming and pressing to make sure it is correct.*** If they are both the same, remove the stitching from one and stitch along the opposite diagonal. Again, check before trimming.

fig. 6
make 1 dark corner block

fig. 7
make 1 of each block

Cutting the Sashing

Remove the selvages from your sashing fabric.
  Cut eight strips 1¼″ x the length of your fabric, approximately 67″.
  These strips will be trimmed and used as the horizontal sashes between the rows.

Use the remainder of your fabric to cut three 8½″ wide strips in the opposite direction, perpendicular to the edges where the selvages were removed. The strips will be 8½″ x approximately 30″.
  Cut the three 8½″ strips into fifty-four 1¼″ x 8½″ rectangles.

Completing the Quilt

Refer to the photo on page 6 to lay out the Sixteen Patch and border blocks. Make horizontal rows, placing 1¼″ x 8½″ sashing strips between the blocks. Do not put a sashing strip on the ends of the rows. Sew the blocks and 1¼″ x 8½″ sashes into rows. Press the seam allowances toward the sashes.

Measure your rows and determine their average length. It should be 61″.

Trim the eight long sashing strips to this measurement. Place the sashing strips between the rows. Complete the quilt top by sewing the rows and long horizontal sashes together. Press all seam allowances toward the sashes.

Quilt, bind, and enjoy!

Making a Larger Quilt

Make a queen size quilt as directed below.
The finished size of this option is 87¼" x 96".
The queen size requires the following fabric:

57 Tan Worms

57 Dark Worms

Sashing	2⅝ yards
Binding	1 yard
Backing	7¾ yards

Cutting and Piecing

Cut *forty-two light and forty-two dark* worms as directed for the smaller size. Use the pieces to make forty-two Sixteen Patch blocks, twenty-one light border blocks, and twenty-one dark border blocks.

Do not cut any 2½" x 8½" rectangles from the remaining fifteen light and fifteen dark worms. Use them to make two Sixteen Patch blocks from each pair of strips (thirty additional blocks).

Make the four corner blocks of the quilt as directed for the smaller size.

Arrange the Sixteen Patch blocks into nine horizontal rows of eight blocks. Place the border blocks around the perimeter.

Remove the selvages from the sashing fabric. Cut ten strips 1¼" x approximately 94". These strips will be trimmed and used as the horizontal sashes between the rows. Use the remainder of the fabric to cut ninety-nine 1¼" x 8½" sashes. Position the sashes and complete the quilt as directed for the smaller quilt.

A Second Larger Size Option

A *generous queen size or a king size coverlet* (finished size 96" x 96") can be made with the following fabric and numbers of blocks:

63 Tan Worms

63 Dark Worms

Sashing	2¾ yards
Binding	1 yard
Backing	8½ yards

Cutting and Piecing

Use *forty-four light and forty-four dark* worms to make forty-four Sixteen Patch blocks, twenty-two light border blocks, and twenty-two dark border blocks.

Do not cut any 2½" x 8½" rectangles from the remaining nineteen light and nineteen dark worms. Use them to make two Sixteen Patch blocks from each pair of strips (thirty-eight additional blocks).

Make the four corners of the quilt as directed for the smaller size.

Arrange the Sixteen Patch blocks into nine rows of nine blocks. There will be one block leftover and not used to complete the quilt. Place the border blocks into position.

Remove the selvage from the sashing fabric. Cut ten strips 1¼" x approximately 98". These strips will be trimmed and used as the horizontal sashes between the rows.

Use the remainder of the fabric to cut the 1¼" x 8½" sashes. Cut 110 sashes. Position the sashes and complete the quilt as directed for the smaller size.

Sweet Sixteen

39½" x 48¼"

Sweet Sixteen

Here is an option for making a fast and fun lap or crib size with Sixteen Patch blocks. It is an interesting way to show off a fabulous focus fabric in the border.

Finished Size of Quilt – 39½″ x 48¼″
Finished Size of Block – 8″

Fabric Requirements

6 Worms or 12 Half-Strips

White	⅝ yard
Border	⅞ yard
Sashing	1¼ yards
Binding	⅝ yard
Backing	1½ yards, more if fabric is narrower than 42″

Cutting

White
  Cut six strips 2½″ wide.

Border
  Cut three strips 8½″ wide.
    Cut these strips into fourteen 6½″ x 8½″ rectangles.
    Use the leftovers of the strips to cut four 6½″ squares.

Piecing the Blocks

Use the white strips and the worms to complete twelve Sixteen Patch blocks. If you are using six worms, make two Sixteen Patch blocks per fabric. If you are using twelve half-strips, cut each white strip into two half-strips, and make one Sixteen Patch block per fabric. For more instruction on piecing the Sixteen Patch blocks, see page 7.

Cutting the Sashing and Completing the Quilt

Remove the selvages from your sashing fabric. Cut five strips 1¼″ x the length of your fabric, approximately 45″. These strips will be trimmed and used as the horizontal sashes between the rows.

Use the remainder to cut sixteen 1¼″ x 8½″ rectangles and eight 1¼″ x 6½″ rectangles. The shorter sashes are used in the top and bottom border rows.

Lay out the blocks in four horizontal rows of three blocks. Place the border fabric rectangles around the perimeter and the 6½″ squares in the corners. Refer to the photo on page 10. Position the sashes and complete the quilt as directed for *Sand and Sea* on page 8.

Quilt, bind, and enjoy!

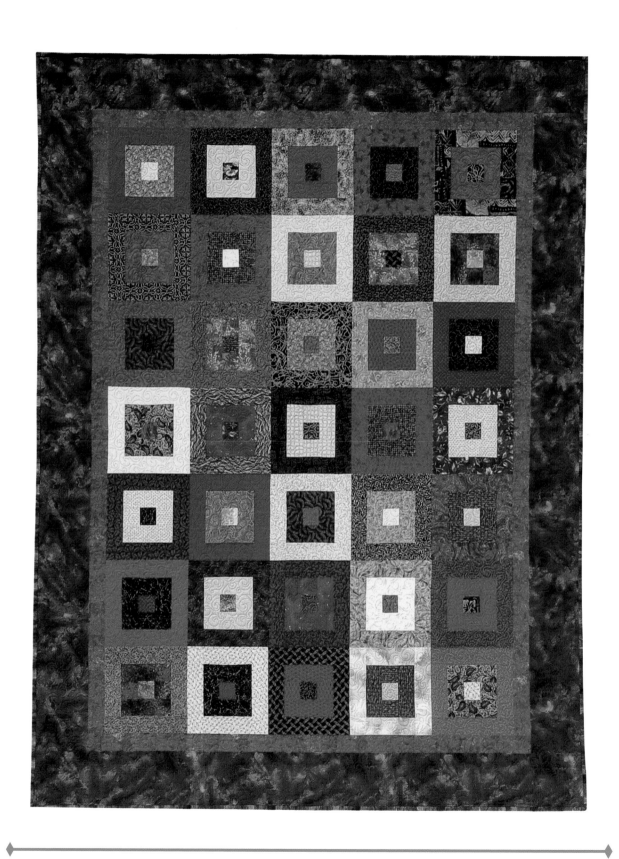

Courthouse Square
67½" x 87½"

Courthouse Square

Courthouse Square and Autumn Evening are two quilts based on the traditional Courthouse Steps block.

Finished Size of Quilt – 67½″ x 87½″
Finished Size of Block – 10″

Fabric Requirements

53 Worms (red, blue, and black)

Inner Border	⅝ yard
Outer Border	2¼ yards
Binding	⅞ yard
Backing	5¼ yards

Cutting

Divide your strips into two piles. Make one pile of eighteen strips. Label these "A". The A fabrics are used as the inner frame around the center squares. Label the second pile of thirty-five strips "B". The B fabrics are used for the outer frame of the blocks. Center squares are cut from both the A and B fabrics.

Cut the following from *each* of the eighteen A fabrics:
four 2½″ x 6½″ rectangles
and five 2½″ squares.

Cut the following from *each* of the thirty-five B fabrics:
two 2½″ x 10½″ rectangles,
two 2½″ x 6½″ rectangles, and
one 2½″ square.

Getting Organized

Set aside one 2½″ square of all fifty-three fabrics. These squares will be the centers of your blocks. This quilt requires thirty-five blocks. You will have some 2½″ squares left.

Before beginning to sew, make thirty-five stacks of pieces, each stack containing the pieces necessary for one block. Each block will use the following pieces:
one 2½″ square for the center (Choose from the fifty-three squares you set aside.),
two 2½″ squares and two 2½″ x 6½″ rectangles of a single A fabric, and
two 2½″ x 6½″ rectangles and two 2½″ x 10½″ rectangles of a single B fabric.

By organizing your fabrics into these stacks before sewing, you can rearrange as many times as you need until you are pleased with all of the blocks' combinations.

Piecing the Blocks

Lay out the pieces for one block as shown in figure 1 prior to sewing.
Sew the pieces together in the following order:

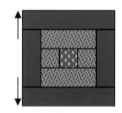

fig. 1
Courthouse Steps block
make 35

Sew the three 2½″ squares together, placing the center square between the two squares of A fabric (figure 2). ***Press the seam allowances away from the center square throughout the construction of the block.***

fig. 2

Sew the 2½″ x 6½″ rectangles of A fabric to the center section (figure 3). Press.

Sew the 2½″ x 6½″ rectangles of B fabric to two opposite sides of the block (figure 4). Press.

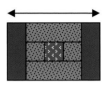

fig. 3

Finally, complete the block by adding the two 2½″ x 10½″ rectangles of B fabric. See figure 1 on page 13. Press.

Completing the Quilt

Arrange the blocks into seven horizontal rows of five blocks. If you rotate every other block a quarter turn, you will not have to match any seam lines except at the corners where the blocks meet. See row 1 and row 2 in figure 5. Make all odd rows like row 1 and all even rows like row 2. Sew the blocks into rows. Press all seam allowances toward the 2½″ x 10½″ rectangles.

fig. 4

Complete the quilt by sewing the rows together. Press the seam allowances to one side.

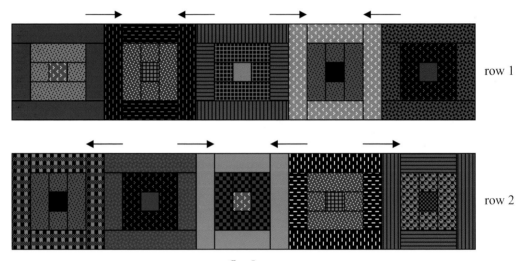

row 1

row 2

fig. 5

Borders

Inner Border

Cut seven 2½″ wide strips, selvage to selvage, from your inner border fabric. Trim the selvages and square the ends of the strips.

Sew two strips end on end to make a piece long enough to fit the side of the quilt. Measure the length of your quilt. Trim the border strip to fit that measurement. Pin and sew the border to one long side of the quilt. Press the seam allowances toward the border. Repeat to add a border to the opposite side of the quilt.

Use one and a half strips to piece a border for the top of the quilt. Trim the border to fit. Pin and sew the border to the top of the quilt. Repeat to add a border to the bottom of the quilt.

Outer Border

Remove the selvages from your outer border fabric. Cut four 7″ wide lengthwise panels, parallel to the edge where the selvages have been removed. These panels may be cut up to 10″ wide to increase the size of the quilt to 73″ x 93″. More backing fabric will be required for a larger quilt. Measure, trim, attach, and press the outer borders in the same way that the inner borders were completed.

Quilt, bind, and enjoy!

Making a Larger Quilt

Make a queen size quilt with fifty-six blocks.
The finished size of this option is 93½″ x 103½″.
The queen size requires the following fabric:

Fabric Requirements

84 Worms

Inner Border	¾ yard
Outer Border	2¾ yards
Binding	1 yard
Backing	8¼ yards

Cutting and Getting Organized

Cut twenty-eight of the worms as directed for "A" in the smaller size. Cut fifty-six of the worms as directed for "B" in the smaller size. Organize them into fifty-six blocks.

Piecing the Quilt

Make fifty-six blocks. Arrange the blocks in eight horizontal rows of seven blocks. Sew the blocks together as directed for the smaller size.

Borders

Add the inner border, using eight strips cut 2½″ wide.

For the outer border, remove the selvages and cut four lengthwise panels 10″ wide. See page 14 for more instruction on borders.

Quilt, bind, and enjoy!

Autumn Evening
43" x 57¾"

Autumn Evening

Here is an option for making a Courthouse Steps quilt with fewer fabrics.

Finished Size of Quilt – 43″ x 57¾″
Finished Size of Block – 10″

Fabric Requirements

Gold (includes sashing)	½ yard
Rust	⅜ yard
Purple	⅝ yard
Setting Triangles	⅞ yard
Border	1⅜ yards
Binding	⅝ yard
Backing	2¾ yards

Cutting

Gold
   Cut one strip 10½″ wide.
      Cut this strip into twenty-four 1″ x 10½″ rectangles.

   Cut one strip 2½″ wide.

Rust
   Cut one strip 6½″ wide.
      Cut this strip into sixteen 2½″ x 6½″ rectangles.

   Cut one strip 2½″ wide.

   Cut one strip 1″ wide.
      Cut this strip into seventeen 1″ squares.

Purple
   Cut one strip 10½″ wide.
      Cut this strip into sixteen 2½″ x 10½″ rectangles.

   Cut one strip 6½″ wide.
      Cut this strip into sixteen 2½″ x 6½″ rectangles.

Setting Triangles
   Cut one strip 16⅛″ wide.
      Cut this strip into two 16⅛″ squares.
         Cut the squares twice, diagonally, making quarter-square triangles. Yield: 8 triangles

   Cut one strip 8⅝″ wide.
      Cut this strip into two 8⅝″ squares.
         Cut the squares once, diagonally, making half-square triangles. Yield: 4 triangles

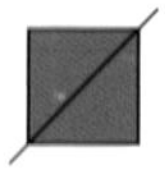

Piecing the Blocks

Cut the 2½ wide strips of gold and rust in half to make two half-strips from each that are approximately 21″ long. Use both pieces of the rust fabric and one piece of the gold to sew a panel like the one shown in figure 1. Press the seam allowances toward the rust fabric. Crosscut the strip-pieced panel into eight sections that are 2½″ wide.

Add the remaining rectangles of rust and purple to these sections as directed on page 14 to complete eight Courthouse Steps blocks (figure 2).

Completing the Quilt

Arrange the eight blocks on point. Use the 1″ x 10½″ gold rectangles for sashing and the 1″ squares of rust for cornerstones. Place the half-square triangles of teal in the corners, and use six of the eight quarter-square triangles for the side triangles. The remaining two setting triangles are not used to complete this quilt.

Figure 3 is an exploded diagram of the quilt. It shows how to construct the rows. Sew the pieces into diagonal rows, and press all of the seam allowances toward the sashing.

NOTE: The first sashing row must be sewn to the first block row before a side triangle will fit. The quilt is completed by making two halves and then sewing the two halves to the center row of sashing. The four corner triangles are added at the end, just before adding the border.

Sew the rows together. Press the seam allowances toward the sashing row.

Borders

Remove the selvages from the border fabric. Cut four lengthwise panels 6½″ wide. See page 14 for more instruction on borders.

Quilt, bind, and enjoy!

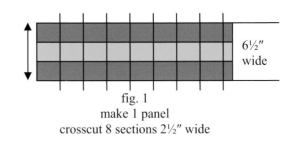

6½″ wide

fig. 1
make 1 panel
crosscut 8 sections 2½″ wide

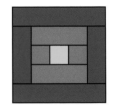

fig. 2
Courthouse Steps block
make 8

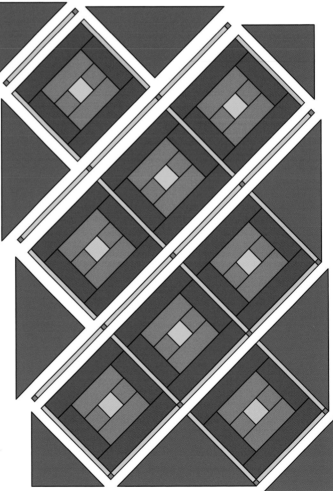

fig. 3
exploded view of
diagonal setting

Grandma's Featherbed
73½" x 79½"

Grandma's Featherbed

Grandma's Featherbed and Bluebonnets are two quilts based on the traditional Grandmother's Pride block.

Finished Size of Quilt – 73½" x 79½"
Finished Size of Block – 8½"

Fabric Requirements

20 Tan Worms

5 Pumpkin Worms

10 Dark Worms (green, purple, burgundy, & brown)

Setting Triangles	1¾ yards
Strip Sashing	1 yard
Border	2¼ yards
Binding	⅞ yard
Backing	5 yards

Cutting

Cut thirteen 2½" squares from *each* of the twenty tan worms.

Cut sixteen 2½" squares from *each* of the five pumpkin worms.

Cut sixteen 2½" squares from *each* of the ten dark worms.

Setting Triangles
  Cut three strips 13¼" wide.
    Cut these strips into eight 13¼" squares.
      Cut the squares twice, diagonally, to make quarter-square triangles. Yield: 32 triangles

  Cut two strips 6⅞" wide.
    Cut these strips into eight 6⅞" squares.
      Cut the squares once, diagonally, to make half-square triangles. Yield: 16 triangles

Getting Organized

Before sewing, make twenty stacks of pieces, each stack containing the pieces necessary for one block.

Each block will use the following pieces:
all thirteen 2½" squares of one tan fabric,
four 2½" squares of one pumpkin fabric, and
eight 2½" squares of one dark fabric.

By organizing your fabrics into these stacks before sewing, you can rearrange as many times as you need until you are pleased with all of the blocks' combinations.

Piecing the Blocks

Lay out the pieces for one block as shown in figure 1. Piece the block by making rows (figure 2). Press all seam allowances in the directions shown by the arrows.

Sew the rows together. Press the seam allowances away from the center row.

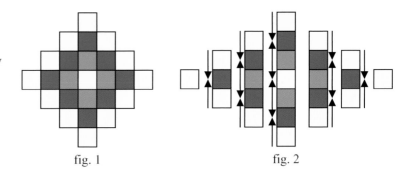

fig. 1   fig. 2

Trim the edges of the block, leaving ¼" seam allowances beyond the corners of the dark squares. See photo 1.

Repeat to complete twenty Grandmother's Pride blocks.

Completing the Quilt

Set five blocks on point in a vertical row. Position eight quarter-square triangles along the sides of the row. Use four half-square triangles for the corners at the top and bottom of the row.

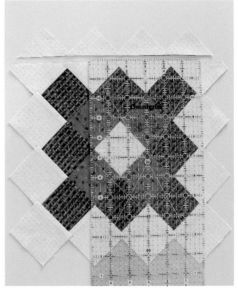

Sew the triangles to the blocks as shown in figure 3. Press the seam allowances toward the triangles. Sew the sections from figure 3 together to make a row. Press the seam allowances to one side. Repeat to construct a total of four rows.

photo 1

Strip Sashing

Remove the selvages from the sashing fabric. Cut fourteen 2½" x approximately 36" strips along the lengthwise grain, **parallel to the edge where the selvages have been removed.** Square the ends of the strips and sew them into pairs to make seven strips that are approximately 70" long.

Determine the average length of your rows. They should be 60½" long. Cut *five* of the pieced sashing strips to fit that measurement. Pin and sew the sashing strips and rows together. Press the seam allowances toward the sashing.

Determine the width of your quilt. It should be 58½" wide. Trim the remaining two sashing strips to fit. Attach a sashing strip to the top and one to the bottom of your quilt. Press the seam allowances toward the sashes.

Border

Remove the selvages from your outer border fabric. Cut four 8" wide lengthwise panels, parallel to the edge where the selvages have been removed. See page 14 for more instruction on borders.

Quilt, bind, and enjoy!

fig. 3

Making a Larger Quilt

Make a queen size quilt with thirty blocks.
The finished size of this option is 91½″ x 95½″.
The queen size requires the following fabric:

30 Tan Worms

8 Pumpkin Worms

15 Dark Worms (green, purple, burgundy, & brown)

Setting Triangles	2½ yards
Strip Sashing	1¼ yards
Border	2¾ yards
Binding	1 yard
Backing	8¼ yards

Cutting

Cut thirteen 2½″ squares from *each* of the thirty tan worms.

Cut sixteen 2½″ squares from *each* of the eight pumpkin worms.

Cut sixteen 2½″ squares from *each* of the fifteen dark worms.

Setting Triangles
  Cut five strips 13¼″ wide.
    Cut these strips into thirteen 13¼″ squares.
      Cut the squares twice, diagonally, to make quarter-square triangles. Yield: 52 triangles

  Cut two strips 6⅞″ wide.
    Cut these strips into ten 6⅞″ squares.
      Cut the squares once, diagonally, to make half-square triangles. Yield: 20 triangles

Piecing and Setting the Quilt

Follow the instructions for the smaller size, but make thirty blocks instead of twenty. Set the blocks on point, making five vertical rows of six blocks.

Set the quilt with strip sashes. Remove the selvages from the sashing fabric. Cut sixteen 2½″ x approximately 45″ strips along the lengthwise grain, parallel to the edge where the selvages have been removed. Square the ends of the strips and sew them into pairs to make eight strips that are approximately 88″ long. See page 21 for more instruction on sashing.

Borders

For the border cut four lengthwise panels 10″ wide, as directed for the smaller quilt. See page 14 for more instruction on borders.

Quilt, bind, and enjoy!

Bluebonnets

62" x 79"

Bluebonnets

Here is an option for making a Grandmother's Pride quilt with fewer fabrics. Using yardage instead of worms allows you to strip piece the blocks.

Finished Size of Quilt – 62″ x 79″
Finished Size of Block – 8½″

Fabric Requirements

White	1¼ yards
Medium Blue	½ yard
Green	⅞ yard
Setting Squares	1½ yards
Border	1⅞ yards
Binding	¾ yard
Backing	4¾ yards

Cutting

White
  Cut fifteen strips 2½″ wide.
    Reserve eleven strips for strip-piecing.
    Use four strips to cut fifty-eight 2½″ squares.

Medium Blue
  Cut five strips 2½″ wide.
    Reserve four strips for strip-piecing.
    Use the remaining strip to cut eight 2½″ squares.

Green
  Cut nine strips 2½″ wide.
    Reserve eight strips for strip-piecing.
    Use the remaining strip to cut sixteen 2½″ squares.

Setting Squares
  Cut five strips 9″ wide.
    Cut these strips into seventeen 9″ squares.

Piecing the Blocks

Use the reserved 2½″ strips to piece and crosscut the panels as shown in figure 1 on page 25.

Use two strips of white and one strip of green to piece an A panel. Press the seam allowances toward the green. Repeat to make a second A panel.

Use two strips of white, two strips of green, and one strip of blue to piece a B panel. Press the seam allowances toward the green. Repeat to make a second B panel.

Use three strips of white, two strips of green, and two strips of blue to piece a C panel. Press the seam allowances in the directions shown by the arrows.

Crosscut all of the panels into sections that are 2½″ wide. Each panel will yield sixteen sections.

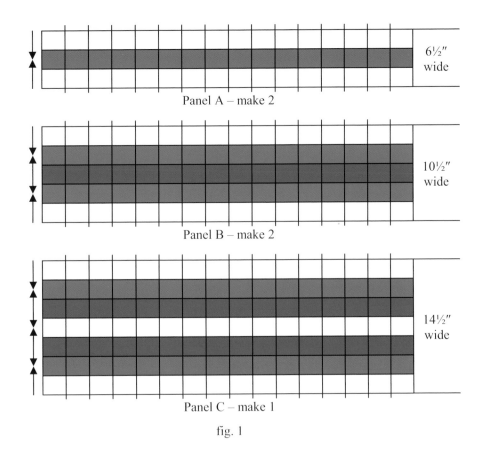

Panel A – make 2

6½″ wide

Panel B – make 2

10½″ wide

Panel C – make 1

14½″ wide

fig. 1

Use all of the crosscut sections and thirty-two squares of white to complete sixteen blocks (figure 2). Press the seam allowances away from the center row. Trim the excess, leaving ¼″ for seam allowance (photo 1 on page 21).

The quilt requires eighteen pieced blocks. Use the remaining squares of all three fabrics to make two more Grandmother's Pride blocks. See page 21 for more detailed instruction.

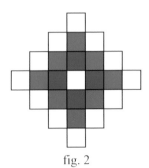

fig. 2

Completing the Quilt

Alternate the pieced blocks with the setting squares, beginning with a pieced block in the upper left corner. Make seven horizontal rows of five blocks. Refer to the photo of the completed quilt on page 23.

Sew the blocks into horizontal rows. Press the seam allowances toward the setting squares. Sew the rows together. Press the seam allowances to one side.

Borders

Remove the selvages from the border fabric. Cut four lengthwise panels 10″ wide. See page 14 for more instruction on borders.

Quilt, bind, and enjoy!

Memory Star
64" x 76½"

Memory Star

Memory Star and Pass the Apple Pie are based on an original variation of the traditional Memory block.

Finished Size of Quilt – 64″ x 76½″
Finished Size of Block – 12″

Fabric Requirements

Each block requires four worms: one tan (background), one bright or medium (inner star), and two dark (outer star). Choose fabrics in sets of four, each set making one block. See figure 1.

20 Tan Worms

20 Bright or Medium Worms (inner stars)

40 Dark Worms (outer stars)

Sashing	⅞ yard
Border	2 yards
Binding	⅞ yard
Backing	3⅞ yards

fig. 1

Cutting Half-Square Triangles and Quarter-Square Triangles

The half-square triangles and quarter-square triangles in this quilt are cut directly from the 2½″ strips, and not cut by the traditional method of cutting squares on the diagonal to generate triangles. To accommodate for the necessary seam allowances, you must use Templates A and B on page 74 or triangle tools. I use the Omnigrid 96 or the Omnigrid 96L, a larger version of the 96, to cut half-square triangles. I use the Omnigrid 98 or the Omnigrid 98L, a larger version of the 98, to cut quarter-square triangles. The Omnigrid triangle tools are numbered with the **_finished size_** of the triangle, not the cut size. If you have another brand of triangle tool, lay it on the respective templates to determine which line to use.

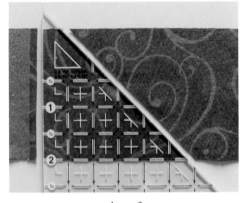

photo 2

Cutting Half-Square Triangles with the Omnigrid 96 or 96L

Trim the selvage from the end of your strip. Align the triangle tool as shown in photo 2. The left edge of the tool is aligned with the squared edge of the fabric, the 2″ line is along the bottom edge of the strip, and the tip of the triangle tool extends ⅛″ beyond the top edge of the strip. Cut along the diagonal.

Rotate your triangle tool 180°, and position it as shown in photo 3. The 2″ line is along the top edge of your strip, the diagonal edge of the tool is in line with the diagonal edge of

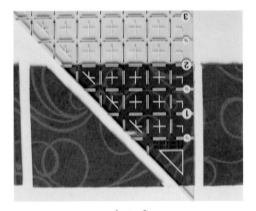

photo 3

the fabric, and the tip of the triangle tool extends ⅜″ beyond the bottom edge of the strip. Cut along the right edge of the triangle tool.

Return to the position in photo 2 to cut a third half-square triangle. Continue alternating between the positions in photos 2 and 3 until you have cut as many half-square triangles as you need.

Cutting Quarter-Square Triangles with the Omnigrid 98 or 98L

Align the triangle tool as shown in photo 4. The 4″ line is along the bottom edge of the strip, and the tip of the triangle tool extends just ⅛″ beyond the top of the strip. Cut along both diagonals.

photo 4

Rotate your triangle tool 180°, and position it as shown in photo 5. The 4″ line is along the top edge of your strip, the left diagonal edge of the tool is in line with the diagonal edge of the fabric, and the tip of the triangle tool extends just ⅛″ beyond the bottom edge of the strip. Cut along the right edge of the triangle tool.

Return to the position in photo 4 to cut a third quarter-square triangle. Continue alternating between the positions in photos 4 and 5 until you have cut as many quarter-square triangles as you need.

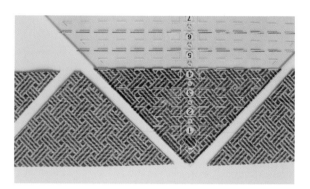

photo 5

Cutting Triangles with the Templates

Duplicate the templates. If you use a copy machine, compare your copies to the original to check for distortion.

Photo 6 shows Template A being used to cut half-square triangles from a 2½″ wide strip. All other templates in this book are used in a similar way.

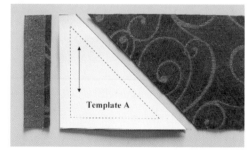

photo 6

Cutting the Memory Star Blocks

All twenty of the tan worms are cut as follows.

Cut these pieces from *each* tan strip:
four 2½″ squares,
eight half-square triangles, cut using the 2″ line on the Omnigrid 96 as directed on page 27 or with Template A, and
four quarter-square triangles, cut using the 4″ line on the Omnigrid 98 as directed above or with Template B.

All twenty of the bright or medium worms are cut as follows.

Cut these pieces from *each* bright or medium inner star strip:
two 2½″ squares and
ten half-square triangles, cut using the 2″ line on the Omnigrid 96 as directed on page 27 or with Template A.

The dark worms should be organized in pairs, one pair for each block. Dark #1 of each pair will be used for the background of the inner star (green in figure 1). Dark #2 will be used for the outer points of the block (blue in figure 1).

All twenty of the dark #1 worms are cut as follows.

Cut these pieces from *each* dark #1 strip:
four 2½″ squares,
two half-square triangles, cut using the 2″ line on the Omnigrid 96 as directed on page 27 or with Template A, and
four quarter-square triangles, cut using the 4″ line on the Omnigrid 98 as directed on page 28 or with Template B.

All twenty of the dark #2 worms are cut as follows.

Cut these pieces from *each* dark #2 strip:
sixteen half-square triangles, cut using the 2″ line on the Omnigrid 96 as directed on page 27 or with Template A.

Getting Organized

REMINDER: Each block requires all of the pieces of four different fabrics, one tan, one bright or medium inner star, one dark #1, and one dark #2. Make twenty piles, each containing the necessary pieces to make one block.

Piecing a Block

Sew a half-square triangle of inner star fabric to a half-square triangle of dark #1. Press the seam allowances toward dark#1. Trim the dog ears. Repeat to make a second unit. See figure 2.

fig. 2
make 2

Sew the units from figure 2 to a square of inner star fabric to make two units like the one shown in figure 3. Press the seam allowances toward the square.

fig. 3
make 2

Sew the two units from figure 3 together to complete the center of the block. Press the seam allowances to one side (figure 4).

fig. 4
make 1

Use the remaining eight half-square triangles of inner star fabric and the four quarter-square triangles of dark #1 to make four flying geese units (figure 5). Press the seam allowances toward the inner star fabric. Trim the dog ears.

fig. 5
make 4

Sew a flying geese unit to two opposite sides of the block center. Press the seam allowances toward the block center (figure 6).

fig. 6
make 1

Sew a 2½″ square of dark #1 to the ends of the two remaining flying geese units. Press the seam allowances toward the squares (figure 7). Sew the units from figures 6 and 7 together to complete the inner star (figure 8). Press the seam allowances in the directions shown by the arrows.

fig. 7
make 2

Use eight half-square triangles of dark #2 and four quarter-square triangles of tan to piece four flying geese units. Press the seam allowances toward dark #2 (figure 9). Trim the dog ears.

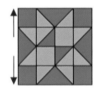
fig. 8
make 1

Sew the remaining half-square triangles of tan and dark #2 together to make eight half-square triangle units. Press the seam allowances toward the dark (figure 10). Trim the dog ears.

fig. 9
make 4

fig. 10
make 8

Use one flying geese unit (figure 9) and two half-square triangle units (figure 10) to piece a section like the one in figure 11. Press the seam allowances toward the flying geese unit. Repeat to complete four sections.

Add a section from figure 11 to two opposite sides of the inner star. Press the seam allowances toward the star (figure 12). Sew a square of tan to both ends of the remaining two sections from figure 11. Press the seam allowances toward the squares (figure 13). Sew the sections from figures 12 and 13 together to complete a Memory Star block (figure 1 on page 27).

Repeat to complete twenty blocks.

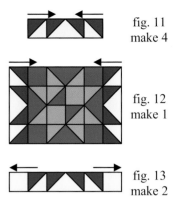

fig. 11
make 4

fig. 12
make 1

fig. 13
make 2

Cutting the Sashing

Remove the selvages from your sashing fabric. Cut twelve strips 1″ x the length of your fabric, approximately 31″. These strips will be used to piece the horizontal sashes between the rows.

Use the remainder of your fabric to cut one strip 12½″ wide in the opposite direction, perpendicular to the edges where the selvages were removed. The strip will be 12½″ x approximately 28″. Cut the 12½″ strip into twenty-five 1″ x 12½″ rectangles.

Completing the Quilt

Lay out the blocks in five horizontal rows of four blocks. Place a 1″ x 12½″ sashing between the blocks and at each end of all horizontal rows. Sew the blocks and sashes into horizontal rows. Press the seam allowances toward the sashes.

Square the ends of the twelve long sashing strips, and sew them into pairs to make six longer sashing strips. Measure your rows and determine their average length. It should be 51″. Trim the six sashes to this measurement. Place the sashing strips between the rows and at the top and bottom. Complete the quilt top by sewing the rows and long horizontal sashes together. Press all seam allowances toward the sashes.

Border

Trim the selvages from the border fabric. Cut four lengthwise panels that are 7″ wide. Panels may be cut up to 10″ wide to increase the size of your quilt to a twin (70″ x 82½″). More binding and backing fabric will be needed for this larger size. See page 14 for more instruction on borders.

Making a Larger Quilt

Make a queen size with thirty blocks.
The finished size of this option is 88½″ x 101″.
The queen size requires the following fabric:

30 Tan Worms

30 Bright or Medium Worms

60 Dark Worms

Sashing	1 yard
Inner Border	1 yard
Outer Border	2⅝ yards
Binding	1 yard
Backing	8 yards

Cutting and Piecing

Follow the instructions for the smaller size to cut and piece the blocks, making thirty blocks instead of twenty. Arrange the blocks into six horizontal rows of five blocks.

Remove the selvages from the sashing fabric. Cut fourteen strips 1" x approximately 36". Use these strips to piece the horizontal sashes.

Use the remainder of the sashing fabric to cut two strips 12½" x approximately 26" wide. Cut these strips into a total of thirty-six 1" x 12½" sashes. Position the sashes and sew the blocks together as directed for the smaller size.

Borders

Add an inner border. Cut eight 3½" wide strips of inner border fabric.

For the outer border cut four lengthwise panels 10" wide. See page 14 for more instruction on borders.

Quilt, bind, and enjoy!

Pass the Apple Pie
53½" x 40"

Pass the Apple Pie

With one Memory Star block and some strip-piecing you can make this patriotic quilt in a matter of hours. Start it on Friday evening and have it done in time for the Sunday barbeque.

Finished Size of Quilt – 53½″ x 40″
Finished Size of Block – 12″, 14″ with frame

Fabric Requirements

7 Red Worms

White	¾ yard
Blue for Star Block	⅜ yard or repeat border fabric
Gold Inner Border	¼ yard
Border & Binding	1½ yards
Backing	1¾ yards, more if narrower than 42″

Cutting

White
  Cut eight strips 2½″ wide.
    Reserve six strips for strip piecing.
    Use the remaining two strips to cut the following pieces:
    six 2½″ squares,
    eighteen half-square triangles, cut using the 2″ line on the Omnigrid 96 as directed on page 27 or with Template A, and
    four quarter-square triangles, cut using the 4″ line on the Omnigrid 98 as directed on page 28 or with Template B.

Blue for Star Block
  Cut two strips 2½″ wide.
    Use these strips to cut the following pieces:
    four 2½″ squares,
    eighteen half-square triangles, cut using the 2″ line on the Omnigrid 96 as directed on page 27 or with Template A, and
    four quarter-square triangles, cut using the 4″ line on the Omnigrid 98 as directed on page 28 or with Template B.
  Cut two strips 1½″ wide.
    Cut these strips into two 1½″ x 12½″ rectangles and two 1½″ x 14½″ rectangles.

Piecing the Block

Use all of the triangles and squares of blue and white to piece one Memory Star block. Refer to figure 1 for the placement of the pieces. Follow the instructions on pages 29 and 30 for piecing and pressing directions.

Use the rectangles of blue to frame the Memory Star block. Sew the 1½″ x 12½″ rectangles to two opposite sides of the block. Press the seam allowances toward

fig. 1

the rectangles. Sew the 1½″ x 14½″ rectangles to the remaining two sides of the star block. Press the seam allowances toward the rectangles.

Completing the Quilt

Use three strips of white and three strips of red to piece a panel like the one in figure 2. Press the seam allowances toward the red fabric. Cut off the selvages and trim this panel to 40″ long.

Use the remaining three strips of white and four strips of red to piece a panel like the one in figure 3. Cut off the selvages and trim this panel to 26″.

Sew the framed star block to the left end of the 26″ panel. Press the seam allowances toward the star block. Sew the 40″ panel to the bottom edge to complete the flag. Press the seam allowances away from the panel containing the star block.

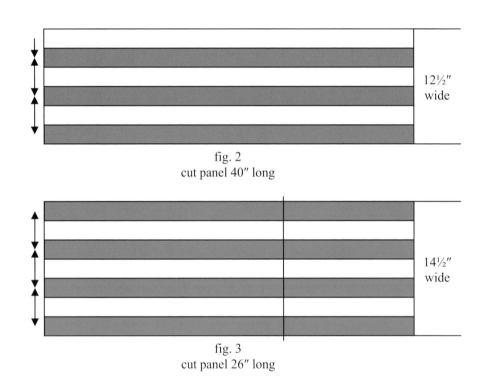

12½″ wide

fig. 2
cut panel 40″ long

14½″ wide

fig. 3
cut panel 26″ long

Borders

Cut four 1¼″ wide strips of gold. Use these strips to add a narrow inner border.

Cut four 6½″ wide strips of blue. Use these strips to add an outer border. See page 14 for more instruction on borders.

NOTE: In an effort to save fabric, the outer border strips are cut across the width of the fabric for this quilt. Because it is a small quilt, there should be no stretching of the borders provided that you measure accurately and trim the borders to fit before attaching them.

Quilt, bind, and enjoy!

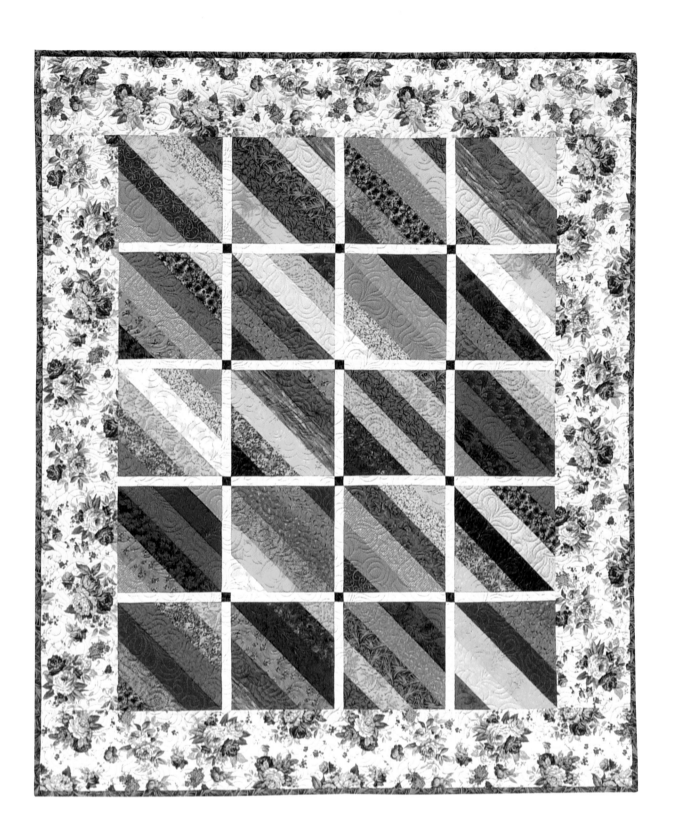

Potpourri
49¾" x 59"

Potpourri

Potpourri and Fish Tales are two quilts from an original design. I found no documentation of this block, but similar traditional blocks are known as Stripes, New Jersey, and, in general, a string quilt.

Finished Size of Quilt – 49¾" x 59"
Finished Size of Block – 8½"

Fabric Requirements

30 Worms or 60 Half-Strips

Sashing	⅜ yard
Cornerstones	1 Worm or a 1¼" wide strip
Border	1½ yards
Binding	¾ yard
Backing	3 yards

Cutting

Cut each of the thirty worms in half to make pieces that are 2½" x approximately 21".
Yield: 60 half-strips

6½" wide

fig. 1 - make 20 panels
Stagger strips by 2".

Piecing the Blocks

Stagger three strips by 2", and sew them together into a panel. See figure 1. Press the seam allowances to one side. Repeat to make twenty panels.

Use the Omnigrid 98L triangle tool to cut pieced quarter-square triangles as shown in photos 7 and 8. Align the bottom of the tool with the bottom edge of the strip pieced panel. The tip of the triangle tool will extend beyond the top edge of the panel by ⅛" (photo 7). If your triangle tool and panel do not align as shown, check your pressing and seam allowances. The panels should measure 6½" wide. Restitch if necessary.

Cut the first triangle. Rotate the triangle tool 180° (photo 8) and cut a second triangle. Cut two triangles from each panel. Yield: 40 triangles

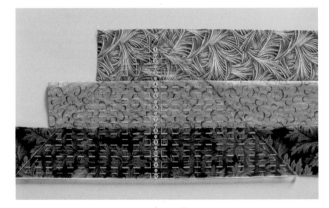

photo 7

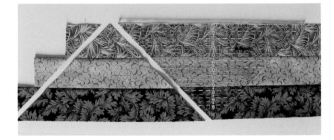

photo 8

NOTE: If you do not have the Omnigrid 98L triangle tool, make a template from a large piece of paper. Cut a 13¼" square. Cut that square twice, diagonally, into four quarter-square triangles. You have four paper templates to use for cutting the pieced quarter-square triangles.

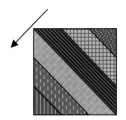

Sew two pieced triangles together along the longest edge (figure 2). Press the seam allowances to one side. **Press carefully to avoid distorting the bias edges.** Trim the dog ears. Repeat to make 20 blocks.

fig. 2
make 20 blocks

Cutting the Sashing and Cornerstones

Cut one 9" wide strip of sashing fabric.
  Cut this strip into thirty-one 1¼" x 9" rectangles.

From the cornerstone fabric cut twelve 1¼" squares.

Completing the Quilt

Refer to the photo of the quilt on page 35 for the layout of the blocks, sashes, and cornerstones. There are no sashes along the outer edges of the blocks, only between them. Sew the pieces into horizontal rows. Press the seam allowances toward the sashes in all rows. Sew the rows together. Press the seam allowances toward the sashing rows.

Border

Trim the selvages from the border fabric. Cut four lengthwise panels that are 7" wide. See page 14 for more instruction on borders.

Quilt, bind, and enjoy!

Making a Larger Quilt

Make a queen size quilt with seventy-two blocks.
The finished size of this option is 92¾" x 102".
The queen size requires the following fabric:

108 Worms

Sashing	1¼ yards
Cornerstones	1 Worm
Border	2¾ yards
Binding	1 yard
Backing	8¼ yards

Cutting

Worms
  Cut each of the 108 worms in half, as directed for the smaller size.

Sashing
  Cut four 9″ wide strips.
    Cut these strips into a total of 127 rectangles that are 1¼″ x 9″.

Cornerstones
  Cut the worm in half, lengthwise, making two 1¼″ wide strips.
    Cut these strips into a total of fifty-six 1¼″ squares.

Piecing the Quilt

Follow the instructions for the smaller size, but make seventy-two blocks instead of twenty. Set the blocks into nine horizontal rows of eight blocks.

Position the sashes and cornerstones, and complete the top as directed for the smaller version.

Border

Trim the selvages from the border fabric. Cut four lengthwise panels that are 10″ wide. See page 14 for more instruction on borders.

Quilt, bind, and enjoy!

Fish Tales

48½″ x 65½″

Fish Tales

Here is an option for making a string quilt with fewer fabrics using the block from *Potpourri*.

Finished Size of Quilt – 48½" x 65½"
Finished Size of Block – 8½"

Fabric Requirements

Gold #1	⅝ yard
Red	⅝ yard
Gold #2	⅝ yard
Dark Blue	⅝ yard
Medium Green	⅝ yard
Dark Green	⅝ yard
Border	1⅝ yards
Binding	¾ yard
Backing	3 yards

Cutting

From **each of the six ⅝ yard pieces** cut six strips 2½" wide. **Do not** cut these strips into half-strips.

Piecing the Blocks

Use the gold and red strips, placing a red strip in the middle between a strip of gold #1 and a strip of gold #2, to make six A panels (figure 1). Stagger the strips by 2". Press the seam allowances in the direction shown by the arrow.

Use the green and blue strips, placing a medium green strip in the middle between a strip of dark green and a strip of dark blue, to make six B panels. Stagger the strips by 2" in the opposite direction. See figure 2. Press the seam allowances in the direction shown by the arrow.

Place a B panel on top of an A panel, right sides together. Make sure that the top strip of the B panel is always on top of the bottom strip of the A panel. If the seams have been pressed correctly they should all nest together.

Sew along both long sides of the pair of panels to make a tube. Do not turn the tube right side out. Repeat to make six tubes.

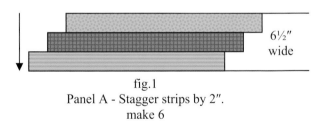

6½" wide

fig.1
Panel A - Stagger strips by 2".
make 6

6½" wide

fig. 2
Panel B - Stagger strips by 2"
in the opposite direction.
make 6

Use the Omnigrid 98L triangle tool or a template (See page 37 for instruction on making a template.) to cut quarter-square triangles from the tubes. Refer to the instructions and photos 7 and 8 on page 36 for alignment. Cut a total of twenty-four triangles, four from each tube.

NOTE: Wide fabrics may yield a fifth block from each tube.

Remove the few stitches from the tip of each triangle. Press the seam allowances in the directions shown by the arrows in figure 3. You will have twelve "X" blocks and twelve "Y" blocks. Trim the dog ears.

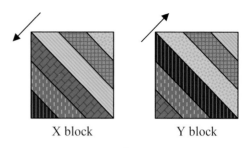

X block   Y block

fig. 3
make 12 of each block

Completing the Quilt

Alternate the "X" and "Y" blocks referring to the photo of the quilt on page 39 for their positions and rotations. Make six rows of four blocks.

Sew the blocks into horizontal rows.

Press the seam allowances of the odd rows to the left.
Press the seam allowances of the even rows to the right.

Sew the rows together. Press the seam allowances to one side.

Border

Trim the selvages from the border fabric. Cut four lengthwise panels that are 7½" wide. See page 14 for more instruction on borders.

Quilt, bind, and enjoy!

Turquoise Trail
49½″ x 57½″

42

Turquoise Trail

Turquoise Trail and Happy Talk are based on a simplification of the block best known as 54-40 or Fight.

Finished Size of Quilt – 49½″ x 57½″
Finished size of Block – 8″

Fabric Requirements

30 Worms

Light Turquoise	⅞ yard
Border	⅞ yard
Binding	¾ yard
Backing	3 yards

Cutting

Cut the following from **each** of the 30 worms:

Cut eleven 2½″ squares.

Use the remainder of the worms to cut four triangles from each, using the 2½″ line on the "Tri" Tool of the Tri-Recs Tool Set or Template C. Position the "Tri" Tool with the 2½″ line at the bottom of the strip as shown in photo 9. Trim along both sides of the tool.

Rotate the "Tri" Tool, place the 2½″ line at the top edge of the strip, and cut as shown in photo 10. Repeat the positions in photos 9 and 10 to cut four triangles from each of the thirty fabrics.

photo 9

photo 10

Light Turquoise

Cut nine 2½″ strips.

Use two strips to cut thirty 2½″ squares.

Use the remaining strips to cut triangles with the "Recs" Tool of the Tri-Recs Tool Set or Template D. *The strips must be folded in half, selvage to selvage when cutting the triangles so that you cut the necessary reverse triangles, too.* Trim the selvages of the folded strip, place the 2½″ line of the "Recs" tool along the bottom edge of the strip, and cut as shown in photo 11.

Trim away the tiny tip of the triangle. See photo 12. This will be important for aligning the triangles when piecing. I find it is easiest to trim each piece as you cut it instead of waiting to do all of them at the end.

Rotate the "Recs" Tool, place the 2½″ line at the top edge of the strip, and cut as shown in photo 13. Again, trim the tip! Repeat the positions in photos 11 and 13 to cut a total of 120 triangles and 120 reverse triangles.

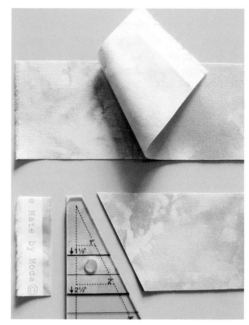

photo 11

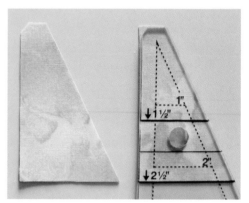

photo 12

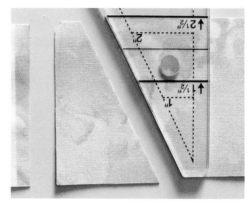

photo 13

Making the Triangle Units

Separate the reverse turquoise triangles from the others. Set aside the 120 reverse triangles. Use the remaining 120 turquoise triangles and the triangles that were cut from the worms to piece units like the one in figure 1. Press the seam allowances toward the turquoise triangles. Look at the unit on the left in photo 14. See how trimming the tip of the turquoise triangle helps with perfect alignment.

Sew the reverse triangles to the second side of the triangles that were cut from the worms. Align them as shown in the unit on the right in photo 14. Press the seam allowances toward the turquoise triangles. See figure 2.

fig. 1   fig. 2
make 120
4 of each fabric

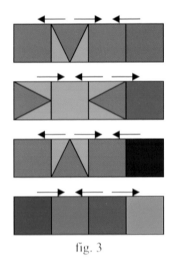

photo 14

Piecing the Blocks

Each block requires the following pieces:
four pieced triangle units from figure 2, all containing the same worm fabric,
four 2½″ squares of worm fabric that match the triangle units,
one 2½″ square of turquoise fabric, and
seven 2½″ squares of worm fabric. These seven fabrics should all be different from each other and different from the worm fabric in the triangle units.

Lay out the block as shown in figure 4. Notice how the four triangle units and the squares of fabric that match them create a single fabric background for the star. The remaining seven squares are positioned along the right edge and the bottom of the star.

Piece the block by sewing the patches into four horizontal rows. Press the seam allowances in the directions shown by the arrows in figure 3.

Sew the rows together. Press the seam allowances in the directions shown by the arrows in figure 4.

Repeat to complete thirty blocks.

fig. 3

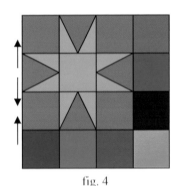

fig. 4
make 30 blocks

Completing the Quilt

Lay out the blocks in six horizontal rows of five blocks. Rotate every other block 180° to create the "trailing stars" pattern. Refer to the photo of the completed quilt on page 42.

Border

Trim the selvages from the border fabric. Cut eight lengthwise panels that are 5″ wide. Trim and square the ends of the panels. Sew the panels into pairs to make strips that are long enough for the borders. See page 14 for more instruction on borders.

Quilt, bind, and enjoy!

Making a Larger Quilt

If you would like to make a queen size quilt from this pattern, I would suggest that you do not use worms. Use strips 3½″ wide to make 12″ blocks, or use strips 4½″ wide to make 16″ blocks. Since this book's focus is worms, I will not go into all the different size possibilities. The Tri-Recs tools come with instructions to help you make many sizes. The quilts on pages 50 and 57 are larger variations of these stars. Consider one of those patterns for a large quilt.

Happy Talk
56¼" x 66¼"

Happy Talk

Here is an option for making a quilt with fewer fabrics using the basic star from Turquoise Trail.

Finished Size of Quilt – 56¾" x 66¼"
Finished Size of Block – 6"

Fabric Requirements

32 Worms to make each star different or 11 Worms to make three stars from each fabric

Background	1¼ yards
Orange Sashing	½ yard
Green Sashing	½ yard
Setting Triangles	⅞ yard
Border	1¾ yards
Binding	¾ yard
Backing	3½ yards

Cutting

Stars

One worm is enough fabric to make three stars. This quilt requires thirty-two stars. Use as many different fabrics as you would like. For **each star**, cut the following:
one 2½" square and
four triangles and four reverse triangles using the 2½" line on the "Recs" Tool as demonstrated in photos 11 – 13 on page 44 or using Template D. ***Remember, the strips must be folded in half, selvage to selvage, when cutting the triangles so that you cut the necessary reverse triangles.***

Background

Cut fourteen strips 2½" wide.
Use eight strips to cut a total of 128 squares (2½").
Use the remaining six strips to cut 128 triangles using the 2½" line on the "Tri" Tool as demonstrated in photos 9 and 10 on page 43 or using Template C.

Piecing the Blocks

Use the background pieces and the star pieces to construct star blocks. Begin by piecing the triangle units shown in figure 1. See page 45 for more details.

Arrange four triangle units, four squares of background, and the center square as shown in figure 2. Complete the block by sewing the units into three horizontal rows. Press all seam allowances toward the squares. Sew the rows together. Press the seam allowances away from the center row.

Make thirty-two star blocks.

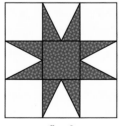

fig. 1
make 128
4 for each block

fig. 2
make 32 blocks

Cutting the Sashing, Setting Triangles, and Cornerstones

Orange
  Cut two strips 6½" wide.
    Cut these strips into forty 1¼" x 6½" rectangles.

Green
  Same as orange

Setting Triangles & Cornerstones
  Cut two strips 10¾" wide.
    Cut these strips into four 10¾" squares.
      Cut the squares twice, diagonally, into quarter-square triangles (side triangles).
      Yield: 16 triangles

    Use the remainder of the 10¾" strip to cut two 6¼" squares.
      Cut these squares once, diagonally, into half-square triangles (corners).
      Yield: 4 triangles

  Cut two strips 1¼" wide.
    Cut these strips into forty-nine 1¼" squares for the cornerstones.

Completing the Quilt

Refer to the photo of the quilt on page 47 to position the blocks, sashes, cornerstones, and setting triangles in an on point setting. There will be two quarter-square triangles left over and not used to complete the quilt.

Sew the quilt together by piecing diagonal rows. See page 18 for more instruction on diagonal setting. Press the seam allowances toward the sashing in all rows.

Sew the rows together. Press the seam allowances toward the sashing rows.

Border

Trim the selvages from the border fabric. Cut four lengthwise panels that are 9" wide. See page 14 for more instruction on borders.

Quilt, bind, and enjoy!

Pink Lemonade
49½″ x 67½″

Pink Lemonade

Pink Lemonade and *Black & White & Stars Allover* are two more original variations based on the 54-40 or Fight block.

Finished size of Quilt – 49½″ x 67½″
Finished size of Block – 12″

Fabric Requirements

16 Yellow Worms

12 Pink Worms or 24 Half-Strips

Pink Stars & Sashing	1 yard
Yellow Cornerstones	1 Worm
Border	1¾ yards
Binding	¾ yard
Backing	3¼ yards

Before You Begin

This pattern uses cutting techniques that are similar to those used in *Memory Star* (half-square triangles on page 27), *Potpourri* (strip-pieced quarter-square triangles on page 36), and *Turquoise Trail* (Tri-Recs tools on page 43). I urge you to read through those patterns to familiarize yourself with the cutting techniques before proceeding to make *Pink Lemonade*. Templates or template making instructions have been provided for you to use if you do not have the tools.

Cutting

Yellow Worms
  Set aside the one yellow worm that will be used for cornerstones. It will be cut later.
  Cut each of the remaining sixteen yellow worms as follows:
    Cut one 2½″ square and one 2½″ x 4½″ rectangle.
    Reserve the remainder of each strip for strip-piecing.

Pink Worms
  Cut each of the pink worms in half, making two pieces 2½″ x approximately 21″ from each.
  Yield: 24 half-strips

Pink Star Fabric
  Cut three strips 4½″ wide.
    Use the strips to cut triangles with the "Recs" Tool of the Tri-Recs Tool Set or Template F. **The strips must be folded in half, selvage to selvage when cutting the triangles so that you cut the necessary reverse triangles, too.** Trim the selvages off the folded strip, place the 4½″ line of the "Recs" tool along the bottom edge of the strip, and cut as shown in photo 15 on the next page.

    NOTE: Trim away the tiny tip of the triangle. See photo 12 on page 44. This will be important for aligning the triangles when piecing. I find it is easiest to trim each piece as you cut it instead of waiting to do all of them at the end.

Rotate the "Recs" Tool, place the 4½" line at the top edge of the strip, and cut as shown in photo 16. Again, trim the tip! Repeat the positions in photos 15 and 16 to cut a total of 32 triangles and 32 reverse triangles.

Cut one strip 2½" wide.
Cut this strip into sixteen 2½" squares.

Piecing a Star Block

One star block requires the following pieces:
all of the pieces of two yellow worms (the 2½" square, the 2½" x 4½" rectangle, and the remainder of the strip),
two 2½" squares of pink star fabric,
four pink star triangles, and
four pink star reverse triangles.

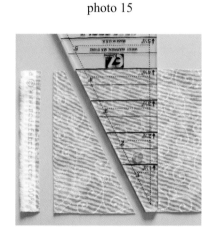

photo 15

Use the four 2½" squares (two pink and one each of the two yellow fabrics) to piece a four patch (figure 1). Sew the squares into pairs. Press the seam allowances toward the pink. Sew the pairs together to complete a four patch. Press the seam allowances to one side.

fig. 1

Sew together the remainder of the two yellow strips to make a panel as shown in figure 2. Press the seam allowances to one side.

Crosscut two sections that are 2½" wide. See figure 3. The remainder of the strip-pieced panel will be used to cut a variety of triangles as directed below. Cut carefully, there is not much excess.

photo 16

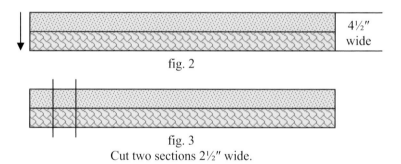

4½"
wide

fig. 2

fig. 3
Cut two sections 2½" wide.

Use the "Tri" tool from the Tri-Recs Tool Set or Template E to cut four triangles. Position the "Tri" tool with the 4½" line at the bottom of the panel as shown in photo 17. Trim along both sides of the tool. Rotate the "Tri" tool, place the 4½" line at the top edge of the panel, and cut. See photo 10 on page 43 for the tool's second position. Again, use the 4½" line. Repeat to cut a total of four triangles from the panel.

NOTE: Two of the triangles will have yellow #1 at the base, and the other two triangles will have yellow #2 at the base. This is correct.

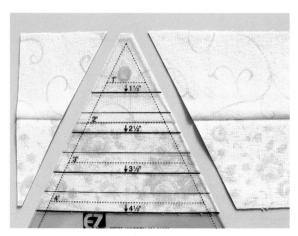

photo 17

52

Square the ends of what is left of the strip-pieced panel. ***Fold it in half so that you will cut the necessary reverse pieces.*** Use the 4″ line on the Omnigrid 96 or 96L half-square triangle tool or Template G to cut two pairs of triangles from the folded strip. See photos 18 and 19. Again, two triangles will have yellow #1 at the base, and two will have yellow #2 at the base.

REMEMBER: If you are using a different brand of triangle tool, compare your tool to Template G to determine which line you should be using.

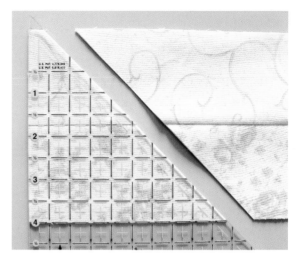

photo 18

Add a 2½″ x 4½″ rectangle of yellow to each of the crosscut sections from figure 3. See figure 4. ***Pay close attention to the positions of the fabrics and the rotation of the sections here and through the completion of the block. They must look exactly like the ones in each figure when complete.*** Press the seam allowances toward the rectangles.

Arrange the four strip-pieced yellow half-square triangles to make the units shown in figure 5. Again, pay attention to the fabric placements. Sew them together. Press the seam allowances to one side. Trim the dog ears.

Use the yellow triangles that were cut with the "Tri" tool, four pink star points, and four reverse pink star points to piece the triangle units in figure 6. Press the seam allowances toward the pink. For more details in aligning and piecing these units see photo 14 on page 45.

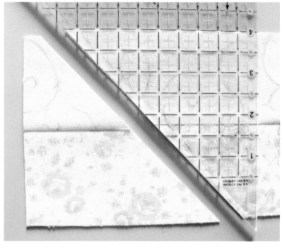

photo 19

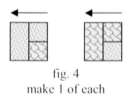

fig. 4
make 1 of each

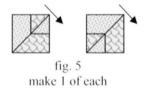

fig. 5
make 1 of each

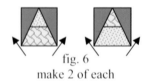

fig. 6
make 2 of each

Arrange all of the pieces from above to complete a star block (figure 7). Sew the block together by making horizontal rows. Press the seam allowances away from the star points. Sew the rows together. Press the seam allowances away from the center row.

Repeat to make eight star blocks.

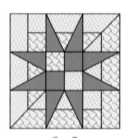

fig. 7
make 8 blocks

Piecing the Pink Setting Triangles

Refer to the instructions on page 36 for strip-piecing and cutting the quarter-square triangles. Piece eight panels of three half-strips as directed. Press. Cut sixteen triangles from the eight panels (figure 8).

Reserve four triangles for the corners of the quilt. Sew the remaining triangles into six pairs to make the side triangles (figure 9). Press the seam allowances to one side.

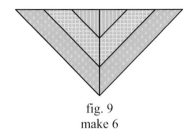

fig. 8
cut 16

fig. 9
make 6

Cutting the Sashing and Cornerstones

Pink Sashing
  Cut one strip 12½″ wide.
    Cut this strip into twenty-four 1¼″ x 12½″ rectangles.

Yellow Cornerstones
  Cut three 2⅜″ squares.
    Cut these 2⅜″ squares twice, diagonally, to make quarter-square triangles.
    Yield: 12 triangles

  Cut seven 1¼″ squares.

Completing the Quilt

Refer to the photo on page 50 and place the blocks on point, leaving space for the sashing and cornerstones. Put the sashes and cornerstones into place. The tiny quarter-square triangles go along the perimeter of the quilt. There will be two triangles leftover and not used in the quilt.

Finally, position the pieced pink setting triangles. Sew the quilt together by piecing diagonal rows. Press the seam allowances toward the sashing in all rows. Sew the rows together. Press the seam allowances to one side. See page 18 for more instruction on diagonal setting.

Border

Trim the selvages from the border fabric. Cut four lengthwise panels that are 7″ wide. See page 14 for more instruction on borders.

Quilt, bind, and enjoy!

Making a Larger Quilt

Make a queen size quilt with thirty-two star blocks and thirty-two strip-pieced quarter-square triangles. The finished size of this option is 91½″ x 109½″.
The queen size requires the following fabric:

64 Yellow Worms

24 Pink Worms or 48 Half-Strips

Pink Stars & Sashing	3¼ yards
Yellow Cornerstones	1 Worm
Border	2¾ yards
Binding	1⅛ yards
Backing	8¼ yards

Cutting

Yellow Worms

Set aside the one yellow worm that will be used for cornerstones. It will be cut later.

Cut each of the remaining sixty-four yellow worms as follows:

Cut one 2½″ square and one 2½″ x 4½″ rectangle.

Reserve the remainder of each strip for strip-piecing.

Pink Worms

Cut each of the pink worms in half, making two pieces 2½″ x approximately 21″ from each.

Yield: 48 half-strips

Pink Star Fabric

Cut twelve strips 4½″ wide.

Use the strips to cut triangles with the "Recs" Tool of the Tri-Recs Tool Set or Template F. ***The strips must be folded in half, selvage to selvage, when cutting the triangles so that you cut the necessary reverse triangles, too.*** Trim the selvages off the folded strip, place the 4½″ line of the "Recs" tool along the bottom edge of the strip, and cut as shown in photo 15 on page 52. Trim away the tiny tip of the triangle. See photo 12 on page 44.

Rotate the "Recs" Tool, place the 4½″ line at the top edge of the strip, and cut as shown in photo 16 on page 52. Again, trim the tip! Repeat the positions in photos 15 and 16 to cut a total of 128 triangles and 128 reverse triangles.

Cut four strips 2½″ wide.

Cut these strips into sixty-four 2½″ squares.

Sashing

Cut three strips 12½″ wide.

Cut these strips into eighty 1¼″ x 12½″ rectangles.

Cornerstones

Cut a 12½″ long rectangle from the worm.

Trim this 12½″ rectangle to 2⅜″ x 12½″, and use it to cut five 2⅜″ squares.

Cut the squares twice, diagonally, to make quarter-square triangles.

Yield: 20 triangles

Cut the remainder of the worm into two strips 1¼″ x approximately 28″.

Use these strips to cut thirty-one 1¼″ squares.

Piecing and Completing the Quilt

For detailed instructions refer to the smaller quilt.

Piece thirty-two star blocks for the queen size.

Make thirty-two strip-pieced pink quarter-square triangle units. See figure 8 on page 54. Reserve four for the corners. Use the remaining twenty-eight units to piece fourteen side triangles as shown in figure 9 on page 54.

Complete the quilt as directed for the smaller quilt. Refer to the photo of *Happy Talk* on page 47 to see how to arrange thirty-two blocks on point.

Border

Trim the selvages from the border fabric. Cut four lengthwise panels that are 10″ wide. See page 14 for more instruction on borders.

Quilt, bind, and enjoy!

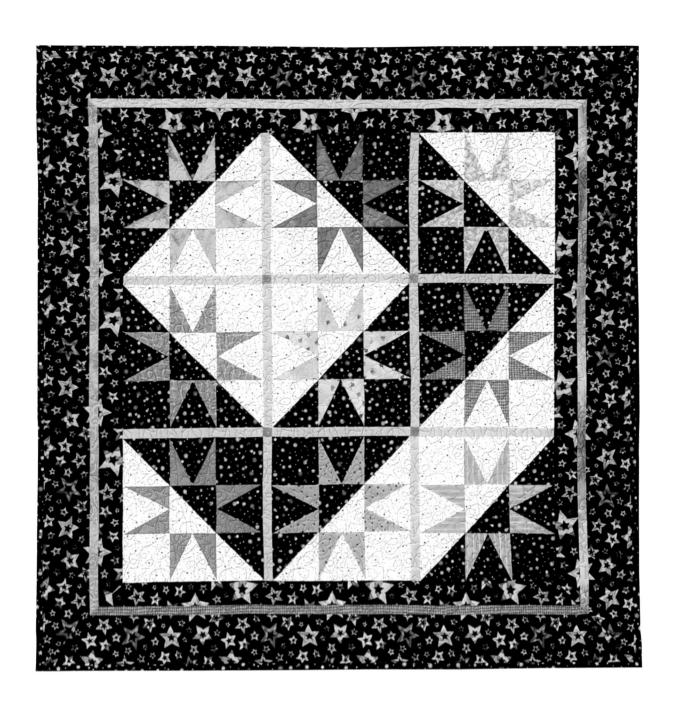

Black & White & Stars Allover

51½" x 51½"

Black & White & Stars Allover

Here is an option for making a quilt based on the 54-40 or Fight block with fewer fabrics.

Finished Size of Quilt – 51½″ x 51½″
Finished Size of Block – 12″

Fabric Requirements

9 Worms for Stars

White Background	⅞ yard
Black Background	⅞ yard
Sashing	½ yard
Cornerstones	4 squares (1¼″)
Accent Borders	4 Worms
Border	1⅝ yards
Binding	⅝ yard
Backing	3¼ yards

Cutting

White Background
  Cut two strips 4⅞″ wide.
    Cut these strips into fourteen 4⅞″ squares.

  Cut three strips 4½″ wide.
    Cut these strips into nine 4½″ squares and
    eighteen triangles using the "Tri" tool on the 4½″ line or Template E. These are cut exactly as directed
    for the *Turquoise Trail* quilt (page 43, photos 9 and 10) except that you use the 4½″ line on the tool
    instead of the 2½″ line.

Black Background
  Same as white background

Cutting the Star Points

Fold a worm in half, selvage to selvage. Cut two pairs of 2½″ x 6″ rectangles from the folded worm. Stack the two pairs of rectangles on top of one another, making a stack of four rectangles. Two of the rectangles are right side up and two are wrong side up. This is correct so that you will have the necessary reverse pieces for the star points.

Place the "Recs" tool of the Tri-Recs Tools Set on the stack of rectangles aligning the 4½″ line and the edge of the tool as shown in photo 20 (or use Template F). Cut along the diagonal and trim the tiny tip. See photo 12 on page 44. Notice that the bottom right corner is slightly blunt. It will not affect the triangle's alignment or fit.

Rotate the remaining fabric 180° and place the tool on it as shown in photo 21. Trim the excess and the tiny tip. Repeat with the other eight star fabrics.

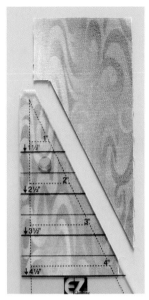

photo 20

Making the Half-Square Triangle Units

Place a 4⅞″ square of white background fabric neatly on top of a 4⅞″ square of black background fabric, *right sides together*. Cut the pair of squares once, diagonally, to make two pairs of half-square triangles. Repeat with the remaining 4⅞″ squares to make a total of twenty-eight pairs. Chain piece twenty-seven of the pairs of triangles along the diagonal edge to make half-square triangle units (figure 1). The last pair of triangles are excess. Press the seam allowances toward the black. Trim the dog ears.

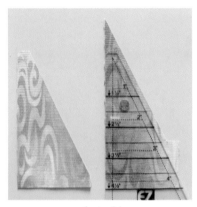

photo 21

Piecing the Blocks

Each block requires the following pieces:
three half-square triangle units from figure 1,
one 4½″ square of white background,
one 4½″ square of black background,
two triangles of white background,
two triangles of black background, and
all eight star points of one fabric.

Use the star points and background triangles to piece the triangle units in figure 2. Press the seam allowances toward the star points. Make two of each unit. See page 45 for more details on piecing these units.

Arrange all of the pieces to make a block (figure 3). Sew the pieces into horizontal rows. Press the seam allowances away from the star points. Sew the rows together. Press the seam allowances away from the center row. Repeat to complete nine blocks.

fig. 1
cut 14 pairs of squares
once, diagonally

make 27 half-square
triangle units

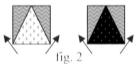

fig. 2
make 2 of each unit
for each star block

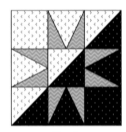

fig. 3
make 9 star blocks

Cutting the Sashing

Cut one strip 12½″ wide.
  Cut this strip into twelve 1¼″ x 12½″ rectangles.

Completing the Quilt Top

Refer to the photo on page 57 and arrange the blocks, sashes, and cornerstones to complete your design. Try other rotations of the blocks. You may prefer a different setting.

Sew the quilt together by making horizontal rows. Press the seam allowances toward the sashing in all rows. Sew the rows together. Press the seam allowances toward the sashing rows.

Borders

Cut one of the worms for the inner border into two 1¼″ x 40″ strips. Trim off the selvages. Piece the two strips end on end to make one long strip. Press the seam allowances to one side. Repeat with the remaining three worms.

Trim the selvages from the outer border fabric. Cut four lengthwise panels that are 7″ wide.

Split one outer border panel lengthwise into two unequal pieces. One piece is cut 2½″ wide, making the second one 4½″ wide. Sew an inner border strip between the two outer border strips. Press the seam allowances toward the outer border. Do not trim the length of this border panel. Center and pin the border panel to one side of the quilt. Sew it to the quilt starting and stopping on the stitching line, ¼″ from each end. Repeat to add a border to the opposite side of the quilt.

Make borders for the remaining two sides of the quilt, but reverse the pressing directions on these borders. Press the seam allowances toward the inner border. Attach the borders to the quilt.

Miter all four corners.

Quilt, bind, and enjoy!

Diamonds are a Girl's Best Friend
42" x 53"

Diamonds are a Girl's Best Friend

Diamonds are a Girl's Best Friend and *Spiraling Pyramids* are original designs based upon the basic 60° equilateral triangle.

Finished Size of Quilt – 42″ x 53″
Finished Size of Block – 6⅞″ x 12″

The setting for *Diamonds are a Girl's Best Friend* is challenging. I hesitate to discourage anyone from making this quilt, but please note that it requires experience in working with many bias edges, on point settings, and odd angles. Read the entire pattern before beginning. It is a project for quilters who want to challenge themselves. Take your time, be accurate, and enjoy the process, or make the much simpler quilt that follows, *Spiraling Pyramids*.

Read all of the instructions to familiarize yourself with this unique quilt before beginning.

Fabric Requirements

18 Worms or 36 Half-Strips

Sashing	1⅝ yards
Setting Triangles & Border	1½ yards
Binding	⅝ yard
Backing	2¾ yards

Strip-Piecing and Cutting the Units

One pair of worms will make two blocks. If you do not want to repeat fabrics, use thirty-six half strips instead of eighteen worms.

Choose one pair of worms (or half strips). Place them right sides together and sew along both long edges forming a tube. Do not turn the tube right side out. Use the 2½″ line on a Creative Grids 60° triangle to cut the tube into units. See photos 22 and 23. Cut nine sections for one block. Cut eighteen sections if you are making two blocks from this pair of fabrics.

NOTE: You may use another brand of 60° triangle tool, but be aware that they are all different. Lay your tool on Template H to determine which is the correct line to use on your tool. If you do not have a 60° triangle tool, use Template H to cut the units.

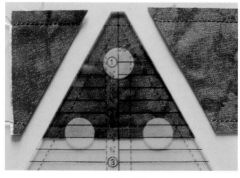

photo 22

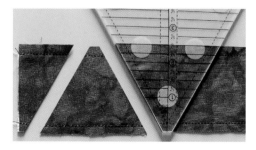

photo 23

Piecing a Block

Remove the few stitches at the top of nine units of one fabric pair. Press the seam allowances of six units toward the dark and three units toward the light (figure 1). Press carefully along the lengthwise grain and handle your pieces gently throughout the construction of the entire quilt to avoid distorting the bias edges.

Arrange the units in three diagonal rows of three units, placing the units that have the seam allowances pressed toward the light in the center row. Sew the units together, making three diagonal rows. Press the seam allowances of the first and third row toward the light fabric. Press the seam allowances of the center row toward the dark fabric. Sew the rows together. Press the seam allowances to one side. See figure 2.

Repeat to complete eighteen blocks.

Cutting the Setting Triangles

Remove the selvages from your border fabric. Cut four panels 5″ wide x the length of your fabric. Reserve these panels for the border.

Use the remainder of your fabric, which is approximately 20″ x 54″ to cut the following.

Cut one strip 14″ x 20″.
  Cut this strip into four 4½″ x 14″ rectangles.

  Fold these rectangles in half. Place the 7″ line of the Creative Grids 60° triangle on the fold as shown in photo 24. ***Notice that the left edge of the fabric rectangle is aligned with the vertical dotted line that is ¼″ left of center on the tool.*** If you are unsure how to align the triangle, or are using a different brand, lay your tool on Template I to check the position. You may use Template I and not a triangle tool to trim the rectangles if you prefer. Trim all four rectangles to make the side triangles.

fig. 1
Press 6 units as shown at left and 3 units as shown at right.

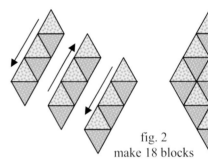

fig. 2
make 18 blocks

photo 24

63

Cut two strips 7½" x 20".
    Use these strips to cut six large equilateral triangles using the 7½" line on the Creative Grid 60° triangle tool. See photo 25. Use Template J to check the position of your triangle tool or use it to cut the large triangles. These triangles fit along the top and bottom edges of the quilt.

Cut one strip 8½" x 20".
    Cut this strip into two 6" x 8½" rectangles.

Stack the rectangles on top of one another, ***wrong sides together***. This will put them into position to cut the necessary reverse triangles. Align the bottom of the Creative Grid 60° triangle tool with the bottom of the rectangle pair and align the left edge of the fabric with the vertical dotted line that is ¼" left of center on the tool. See photo 26. Cut along the diagonal.

Rotate the fabric that was trimmed away 180°, reposition the triangle tool as shown in photo 27, and trim the second pair of triangles. Use Template K to check the position of your triangle tool, or use it to cut the large triangles. These four triangles are the corners of the quilt.

Cutting the Sashing

Remove the selvages from your sashing fabric. Cut ten strips 1½" wide x the length of your fabric. This is the opposite direction from most strip cutting. The straight of grain will be very helpful when dealing with the odd angles and bias edges.

NOTE: The 1½" x 9" rectangles are sewn between the blocks when making the diagonal rows. The other pieces are used as sashing between the rows when sewing the rows together. With accurate piecing the sizes listed will fit, however, if you want a little more excess, you may cut them an inch or two longer. There is plenty of fabric allowed.

Use the strips to cut the following pieces:
one 1½" x 52",
two 1½" x 44",
two 1½" x 28",
two 1½" x 12", and
twenty-four 1½" x 9" rectangles.

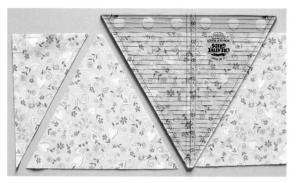

photo 25

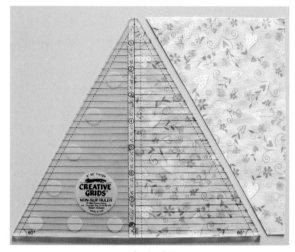

photo 26

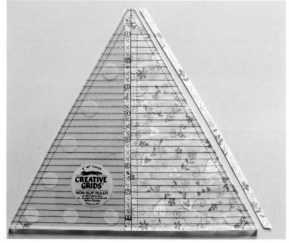

photo 27

Completing the Quilt

Refer to the photo on page 61, and lay out the blocks. Leave some space for the sashing as you position the blocks. ***Set aside the four corner triangles.*** They will be added at the end, just before the border. Place the other setting triangles into position.

Here comes the challenging part!

Row 1 – Sew a 1½″ x 9″ rectangle of sashing to the upper right and lower left sides of the first diamond block. See photos 28 and 29 for the relative positions of the block and sashing.

NOTE: At the wide angle of the diamond block the sashing extends about ¼″ beyond the block (photo 28), and at the sharp angle of the diamond block the sashing extends an inch or more beyond the block. Press the seam allowances toward the sashing.

Lay a ruler along the edge of the block and trim away the excess of the sashing strips as shown in photo 30.

Center a 1½″ x 12″ sashing piece with the upper left edge of the first block, and allow the excess to extend on both ends. The sashing will extend 1″ or more on both ends. Be very careful not to stretch the blocks as you pin them to the sashes. Sew the sashing to the row. Press the seam allowances toward the sashing. Trim the sashing in line with the block's edge. Your piece should look like figure 3 when finished.

Sew the appropriate setting triangles to the upper right and lower left ends of this first row. Press the seam allowances toward the setting triangles.

photo 28

photo 29

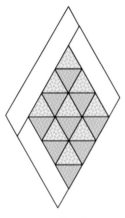

fig. 3

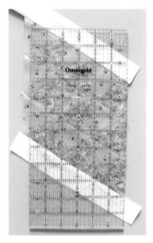

photo 30

Row 2 – Sew a 1½″ x 9″ rectangle of sashing to the **upper right edge only** of the three blocks in the second diagonal row. Press the seam allowances toward the sashing. Trim as before. Sew the blocks together. Add one more rectangle of sashing to the lower left edge of the last block. Press the seam allowances toward the sashing and trim.

Center a 1½″ x 28″ sashing piece with the upper left edge of row 2. Pin, stitch, and press the seam allowances toward the sashing. Trim the edges. Row 2 should look like figure 4 at this point.

Sew the appropriate setting triangles to each end to complete row 2. Press the seam allowances toward the setting triangles.

Make the third diagonal row. The third row contains five blocks and six 1½″ x 9″ sashes.

Center a 1½″ x 44″ sashing piece with the upper left edge of row 3. Pin, stitch, and press the seam allowances toward the sashing. Trim the edges.

Sew the setting triangle to the upper right end to complete row 3. Do not sew a triangle to the lower left end of the row. A corner triangle will be sewn in this position after all the rows have been sewn together and just before the border is added. Press the seam allowances toward the setting triangle.

Pin row 1 to row 2. Align the sashes on the upper right and lower left edges of the diamond block in row 1 with the sashes between the blocks in row 2 so they form straight diagonal lines. Remember to account for the seam allowances. It is helpful to pin the pieces along the seam line and open them to check the positions. Once you are happy with their placement, stitch. Check your work. If the sashes align, press the seam allowances toward the sashing.

Add row 3. Press the seam allowances toward the sashing.

Rotate the whole quilt 180° (or stand at the opposite end of the quilt if it is on a table or the floor), and you will see from this position that you can piece row 6 just like you did row 1, row 5 like row 2, and row 4 like row 3. Sew these rows together to complete the second half of the quilt.

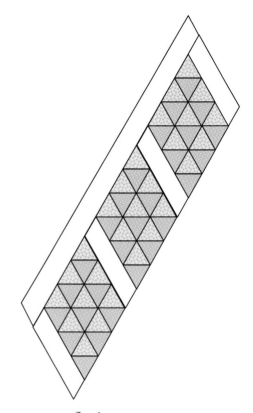

fig. 4

Once you have pieced both halves of the quilt. Sew the two halves to opposite sides of the 1½″ x 52″ sashing strip, aligning the sashing in the rows as you have all along. The ends will offset by 1″ as shown in photo 31. Press the seam allowances toward the sashing. After both halves have been sewn to the sash and pressed, trim the ends (photo 32).

Add the four corner triangles. Press the seam allowances toward the corners. Trim the dog ears.

Border

Use the reserved 5″ wide panels for the border. See page 14 for more instruction on borders.

Quilt, bind, and enjoy!

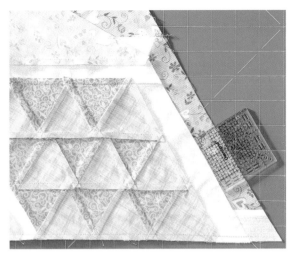

photo 31

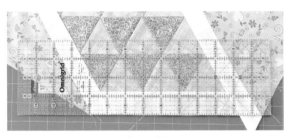

photo 32

Making a Larger Quilt

I suggest that before jumping into a bed size quilt that you make a sample of at least five blocks to test the pattern. A five block quilt will give you the experience of every part of constructing this quilt in any size. It makes a wall quilt, approximately 17″ x 30″ before borders. I am sure that if you are experienced enough to make this quilt, you will have no trouble increasing its size to whatever size you desire. Just remember, one pair of worms will make two blocks.

Spiraling Pyramids
37½″ x 51¾″

Spiraling Pyramids

Here is an option for making a much simpler 60° triangle quilt with fewer fabrics.

Finished Size of Quilt – 37½″ x 51¾″
Finished Size of Block – 8″ high x 9¼″ at the base

Fabric Requirements
9 Worms or 18 Half-Strips

Beige Background	1⅛ yards
Setting Fabric	1½ yards, includes border
Binding	⅝ yard
Backing	2½ yards

Cutting
Beige Background
  Cut thirteen strips 2½″ wide.
    Reserve nine strips for strip-piecing.

    Use the 2½″ line on a Creative Grids 60° triangle to cut the remaining four strips into triangles. Cut a total of seventy-two triangles. The triangles are cut from the strips as shown in photos 22 and 23 on page 62.

    NOTE: You may use another brand of 60° triangle tool, but be aware that they are all different. Lay your tool on Template H to determine which is the correct line to use on your tool. If you do not have a 60° triangle tool, use Template H to cut the triangles.

Strip-Piecing the Units
If you are using half-strips, cut the strips of background fabric in half, making two half-strips that are 2½″ x approximately 21″ from each. Yield: 18 half-strips

Sew one strip (or half-strip) of background to one strip (or half-strip) of worm fabric, right sides together, along both long edges, making a tube.

Do not turn the tube right sides out. Use the 2½″ line on a Creative Grids 60° triangle to cut units from the tube. Again, the units are cut from the tubes as shown in photos 22 and 23 on page 62.

Cut twelve units from each tube if you are using nine worms. Cut six units from each tube if you are using eighteen half-strips.

Piecing a Block

One block requires six pieced units and four triangles of background fabric.

Remove the few stitches at the top of each unit. Press the seam allowances of four units toward the dark and two units toward the background. Press carefully and in the direction of the lengthwise grain throughout the construction of this quilt so you do not distort the bias edges. See figure 1.

fig. 1
Press 4 units as shown
at left and 2 units as
shown at right.

Arrange the six units and four background triangles, placing the triangles at the bottom of each row, in diagonal rows to make a block (figure 2). The units that have the seam allowances pressed toward the background fabric should be in the second row from the left.

Sew the units into diagonal rows. The seam allowances of the first and third row should be pressed toward the background. The seam allowances of the second row should be pressed toward the dark. Sew the rows together and press the seam allowances to one side.

Repeat to make eighteen blocks.

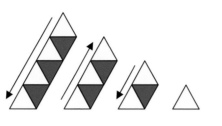 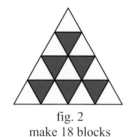

fig. 2
make 18 blocks

Cutting the Setting Triangles

Cut four strips 8½″ wide.
  Use two strips to cut a total of four 5⅛″ x 8½″ rectangles and four 6″ x 8½″ rectangles.

  Set the four 5⅛″ x 8½″ rectangles aside for later use.

  Stack two 6″ x 8½″ rectangles on top of one another, ***wrong sides together***. This will put them into position to cut the necessary reverse triangles. Align the bottom of the Creative Grid 60° triangle tool with the bottom of the rectangle pair and align the left edge of the fabric with the vertical dotted line that is ¼″ left of center on the tool. See photo 26 on page 64. Cut along the diagonal. Rotate the fabric that was trimmed away 180°, reposition the triangle tool as shown in photo 27 on page 64, and trim the second pair of triangles. Use Template K to check the position of your triangle tool, or use it to cut the large triangles. These right triangles will be used to square the rows after the 60° triangles have been sewn together.

Use the remaining two strips to cut fourteen large equilateral triangles using the 8½″ line on the Creative Grid 60° triangle tool. These are cut the same way as those in photo 25 on page 64, except that you use the 8½″line (bottom of the tool) to measure. Use Template L to check the position of your triangle tool or use it to cut the large triangles.

Completing the Quilt Top

Arrange five pieced blocks, four large 60° triangles, and the necessary two right triangles to form a row like the one in figure 3. Sew the blocks together, pressing all of the seam allowances toward the setting triangles. Repeat to make a second row.

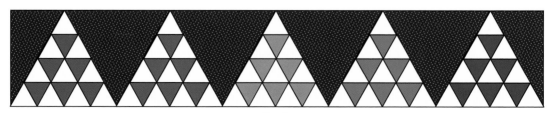

fig. 3
make 2 rows

70

Arrange four pieced blocks, three large 60° triangles, two right triangles, and two 5⅛″ x 8½″ rectangles (one on each end) to form a row like the one in figure 4. Press all of the seam allowances toward the setting fabric.

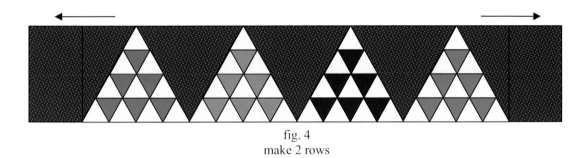

fig. 4
make 2 rows

The rows you have pieced are positioned vertically to complete the quilt. Refer to the photo of the quilt on page 68, and lay out your four rows. Sew the rows together. Press the seam allowances to one side.

Border

Because this is such a small quilt and the borders are so narrow, borders may be cut selvage to selvage. Cut five strips 3″ wide. Use three strips to piece the two side borders. Use the remaining two strips for the top and bottom borders. See page 14 for more instruction on borders.

Quilt, bind, and enjoy!

Final Thoughts

Yardage Calculations

Throughout the book I have designed patterns for quilts that are made with many fabrics and others that are made with few. Even so, I think it is important that you are able to make your own adjustments.

Let's say that you want to make all of the blocks in Grandma's Featherbed from the same three fabrics instead of making all of the blocks different. The original fabric requirements are listed as follows:

20 Tan Worms

5 Pumpkin Worms

10 Dark Worms

How much yardage of each fabric do you need to make all of the blocks from one tan, one pumpkin, and one dark fabric?

Simply multiply the number of worms by 2½″, and that will tell you how many inches of fabric are required. For example, you need twenty tan worms.

$$20 \times 2\frac{1}{2}″ = 50″$$

Divide the number of inches by 36 to determine the number of yards you need.

$$50″ \div 36 = 1.39, \text{ or approximately } 1\frac{1}{2} \text{ yards}$$

Allow extra for preshrinking, straightening, and narrow yardage. I would buy 1¾ yards of tan.

Bed Size Quilts

Not every quilt needs to be a bed size, nor does every quilt that is not a bed size need to hang on a wall. There are many ways to use quilts throughout your home. Here are just a few ways that you might use quilts in a guest bedroom:

- Use a small quilt as a topper on a bed that is fitted with a neutral color comforter, bedspread, or coverlet.
- Fold one or more small quilts and lay them across the foot of the bed. Fold a lap size into thirds, lengthwise, and it will fit nicely across a queen size bed.
- Fold or roll a quilt, tie it in the middle like a package or on the ends with decorative ribbon or a sash of fabric to make a "pillow".
- Drape a quilt over the footboard of the bed or the back of an easy chair or rocker.
- Stack folded quilts on a trunk or bench at the foot of the bed.
- Use a table runner as a dresser scarf or on a bench seat.

Now, move to another room and brain-storm more possibilities.

So, you still want to make bed size quilts. Your queen size bed and mine may be quite different. Use the worksheet on the following page to calculate the desired size of your quilt.

Keep the following things in mind as you plan:

- Do you have a footboard? If so, you may not want your drop to be any longer than the depth of your mattress.

- Do you plan to use pillow shams? If so, you probably want to omit the pillow tuck.

- Is yours a thick, pillow top mattress? If so, you need more drop on the sides and bottom of the quilt.

- Did you preshrink your fabric? If not, you may want to add as much as 10% to both the width and the length of your quilt. Fabric shrinks 4% on the average, and quilting takes up another 2% to 5%, depending upon the loft of the batting and the amount of quilting.

Standard Mattress Size

Here are the USA standard mattress sizes. These measurements are for the top only.

Depth varies greatly depending upon whether the mattress is new or old, and whether it is firm, plush, or pillow top. For the best results, measure the mattress you are trying to fit.

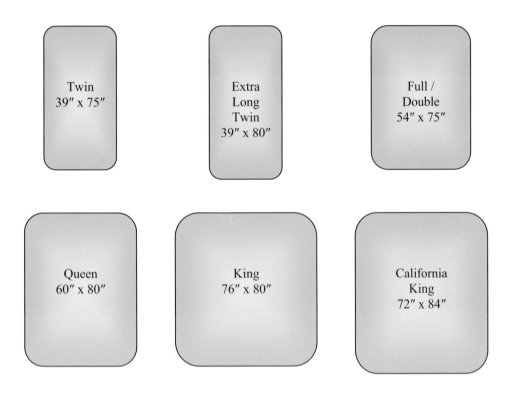

Twin
39″ x 75″

Extra Long Twin
39″ x 80″

Full / Double
54″ x 75″

Queen
60″ x 80″

King
76″ x 80″

California King
72″ x 84″

	Width	Length
Mattress Measurement		
Desired Side Drop x 2		
Desired Foot Drop		
Optional 9″ Pillow Tuck		
Add above measurements to get the ideal finished size.		
Add 5% to 10% for quilting and shrinkage.		
Planned Quilt Size		

Templates

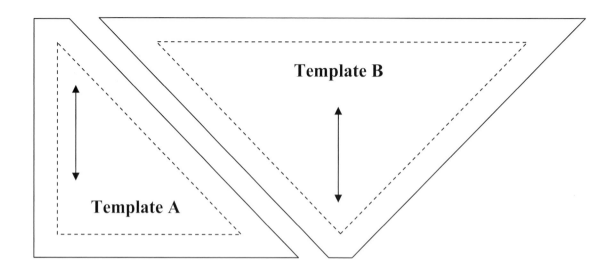

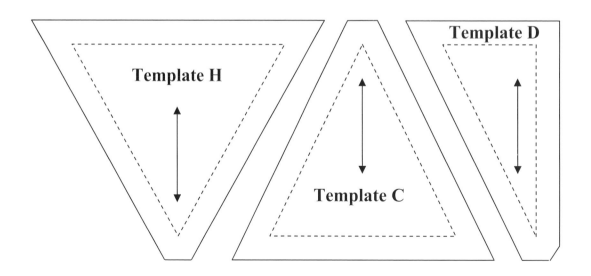

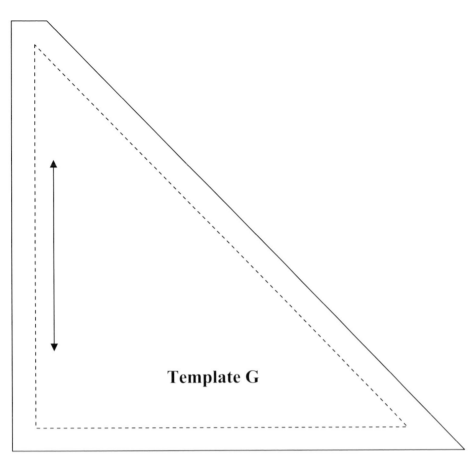

Template G

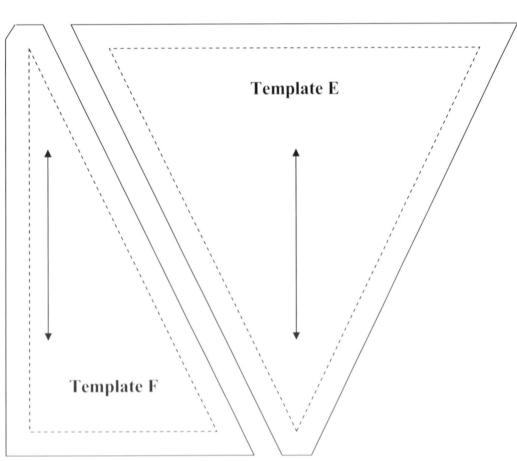

Template E

Template F

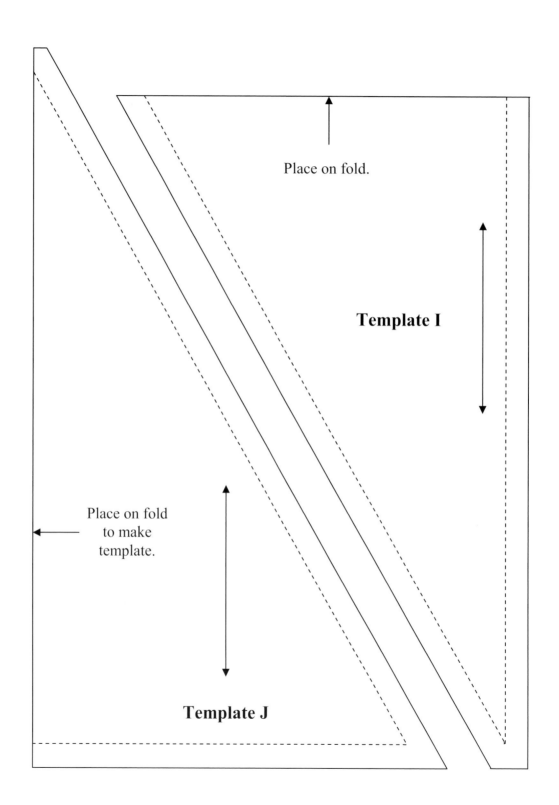

Place on fold.

Template I

Place on fold
to make
template.

Template J

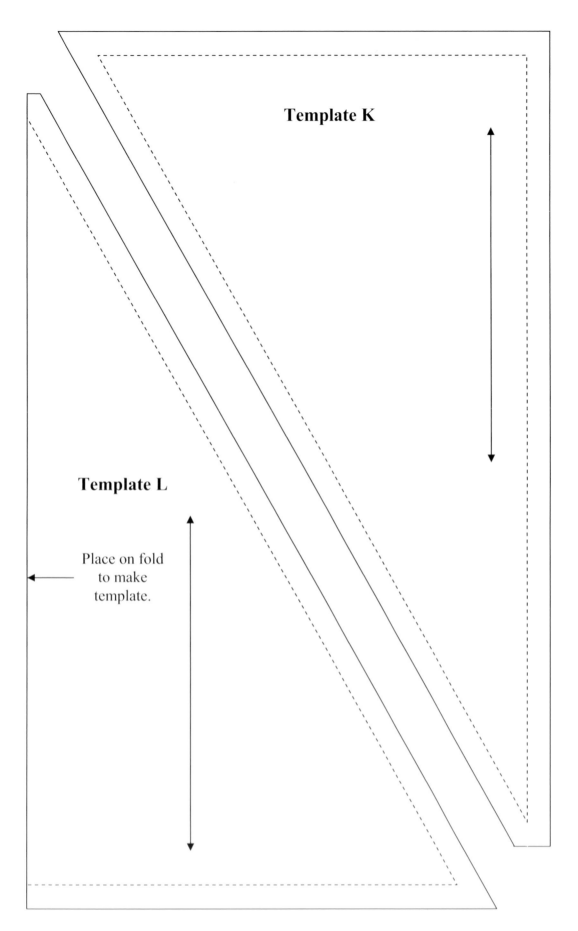

Template K

Template L

Place on fold
to make
template.

Notes

Notes

About the Author

- ❖ Began quilting in 1983, sewing has been a lifelong passion

- ❖ Has taught quilting classes since 1983

- ❖ Published dozens of quilt patterns since 1993, including a new state of the art, full-color line called "Classy Patterns" that is growing fast

- ❖ Wrote and self-published ten books – *An Alaskan Sampler*, 1995; *Blocks and Quilts Everywhere!*, 1997 (out of print); *Scraps to You, Too*, 1998; *Quilting Season*, 1999; *Open a Can of Worms*, 2000; *Noodle Soup*, 2001; *Shape Up Your Fat Quarters*, 2002 (out of print); *Power Cutting*, 2003; *Power Cutting, Too*, 2004; *Another Can of Worms*, 2006

- ❖ Designed and published more than 125 mystery quilt patterns in various formats

- ❖ Wrote many freelance magazine articles

- ❖ Appeared on two episodes of HGTV's *Simply Quilts*, #542 and #615

- ❖ Can be seen in *Quilter's Coffee* episodes on www.quiltersnewsnetwork.com

- ❖ Travels nationally and internationally to teach and lecture for conferences, shops, and guilds

- ❖ Hosts *Spirit of the West* private quilting retreats near her home south of Santa Fe, New Mexico

Learning about the rotary cutter and quilting in 1983 really "opened a can of worms"! In just a few months Debbie Caffrey began teaching quilting at the community school when her teacher moved away.

Debbie has always enjoyed all sorts of puzzles. Math and geometry were favorite subjects in school. So, it was very easy for her to visualize shapes in fabric. When Debbie could not find a pattern for what she imagined, she designed it herself. Linda Liebeg, the owner of the local quilt shop where Debbie taught, became tired of telling customers that there were no patterns for her designs. In her 1993 spring newsletter, she announced, "Debbie Caffrey will have her first pattern available during our sale on Saturday." The only problem was that she hadn't told Debbie! That began the publishing career.

After their three children had grown and moved from Alaska to the Lower 48, Debbie and her husband Dan returned to New Mexico in 2000. They live south of Santa Fe near a movie ranch. If you want to know what it looks like around their house, just watch a few movies – *Silverado*, *The Cheyenne Social Club*, and the Indian village and Old West town scenes of the *Into the West* mini-series filmed in 2005 to name a few.

Debbie travels to teach frequently.
Check the schedule online at
www.debbiescreativemoments.com
to see when your path may cross hers.